UNIVERSITY CASEBOOK SERIES®

2022 SUPPLEMENT TO
FAMILY LAW

CASES AND MATERIALS

UNABRIDGED AND CONCISE
SEVENTH EDITIONS

JUDITH AREEN
Emeritus Professor of Law, Georgetown University Law Center, and
Executive Director, Association of American Law Schools

MARC SPINDELMAN
Isadore and Ida Topper Professor of Law
Michael E. Moritz College of Law
The Ohio State University

PHILOMILA TSOUKALA
Professor of Law
Georgetown University Law Center

SOLANGEL MALDONADO
Eleanor Bontecou Professor of Law
Seton Hall University School of Law

SUPPLEMENT

by
MARC SPINDELMAN
SOLANGEL MALDONADO
PHILOMILA TSOUKALA

FOUNDATION
PRESS

University Casebook Series is a trademark registered in the U.S. Patent and Trademark Office.

© 2021 LEG, Inc. d/b/a West Academic
© 2022 LEG, Inc. d/b/a West Academic
    444 Cedar Street, Suite 700
    St. Paul, MN 55101
    1-877-888-1330

Printed in the United States of America

ISBN: 978-1-63659-950-2

The authors would like to thank Marcus Andrews (Ohio State), Rachel Forman (Seton Hall), Renier Halter-Rainey (Ohio State), and Jonathan Ross (Seton Hall), along with Suzanne Miller (Georgetown Law Library), for various forms of assistance in preparing this Supplement.

TABLE OF CONTENTS

TABLE OF CASES.. VII

Chapter 1. An Introduction to Family Law 1
B.   Structuring Family Law: Some Approaches 1
    3.   Conservative Critique 1
         Fulton v. City of Philadelphia 1
         Note 14

Chapter 2. Marrying 17
B.   Restrictions on Who May Marry 17
    1.   Constitutionality of Marriage Restrictions 17
    2.   Traditional Restrictions...17
         b.   Age...17

**Chapter 3. Marriage: Legal Visions of Privacy, Equality, and
    Violence**..23
B.   Challenges to the Traditional Marriage Model........................23
    1.   Economic and Social Changes 23
    2.   Legal Limits on Sex Discrimination 24
         b.   Positive Law Limits on Sex Discrimination 24
              i.   Title VII...24
                    Bostock v. Clayton County, Georgia................24
                    Note 42
C.   The Doctrine of Family Privacy, Again 43
    1.   The Constitutional "Right to Privacy" (a.k.a. Constitutionally-
         Protected "Liberty")..43
         Dobbs v. Jackson Women's Health Org. 43
         Notes 73

Chapter 4. Parenting..75
A.   Parental Authority and Its Limits...75
    1.   Education..75
    4.   Child Neglect and Abuse 75
         a.   Defining Neglect..79
         b.   Religious Practice or Neglect? 81
D.   Adoption..82
    3.   Standards...82
         c.   Adoption of Native American Children................82
         d.   Sexual Orientation 87
              Fulton v. City of Philadelphia 87

Chapter 6. Assisted Reproductive Technologies and the Law 89
D.   Disposition of Gametes and Embryos...89

Chapter 8. Custody 91
C.   Applying the Best Interests Standard.......................................91
    3.   Race and Ethnicity 91
    5.   Religion 92

G. Modification..93
    1. Change in Circumstances..93
I. De Facto Parents...96

**Chapter 10. Family Law Jurisdiction, Recognition, and Choice
    of Law**..99
D. Custody Jurisdiction..99
    2. International Custody Disputes...99
        Monasky v. Taglieri 99
        Notes 108
        Golan v. Saada 109
        Notes 116

TABLE OF CASES

The principal cases are in bold type.

Abbott v. Abbott, 106, 109
Adams v. School Bd. of St. Johns Cty., 40
Adoptive Couple v. Baby Girl, 83
Agostini v. Felton, 66
Blondin v. Dubois (Blondin I), 109
Blondin v. Dubois (Blondin II), 109
Board of Comm'rs, Wabaunsee Cty. v. Umbehr, 5
Bostock v. Clayton County, Georgia, 24
Boy Scouts of America v. Dale, 13
Brackeen v. Bernhardt, 83
Brackeen v. Haaland, 83, 87
Brackeen v. Zinke, 83
Bray v. Alexandria Women's Health Clinic, 44
Burlington N. & S. F. R. Co. v. White, 26
Bush v. Vera, 72
Carey v. Population Services Int'l, 48
Chafin v. Chafin, 102, 115, 117
Cherokee Nation v. Nash, 84
Christie BB. v. Isaiah CC., 91
Church of Lukumi Babalu Aye, Inc. v. Hialeah, 3
Churchill/Belinski, In re, 94
Cohen v. Cohen, 92
Cooper, State v., 46
Corbitt v. Taylor, 40
Dickerson v. United States, 65
District of Columbia v. Heller, 46
Dobbs v. Jackson Women's Health Org., 43, 90
Doe v. Boyertown Area School Dist., 40
Eckel v. Conover, 97
Edmo v. Corizon, Inc., 40
Eisenstadt v. Baird, 48, 58, 60
Elk Grove Unified Sch. Dist. v. Newdow, 93
Employment Div., Dept. of Human Resources of Ore. v. Smith, 8, 9
Engquist v. Oregon Dept. of Agriculture, 5
F.F. v. State, 81
Ferguson v. Skrupa, 55
Florida Dept. of Health and Rehabilitative Servs. v. Florida Nursing Home Assn., 67
Flynn, Interest of, 19
Fulton v. City of Philadelphia, 1, 87
G. G. v. Gloucester Cty. School Bd., 40
Gambla, In re Marriage of, 91
Garcetti v. Ceballos, 5

Geduldig v. Aiello, 44
Gibbons v. Ogden, 43
Glenn v. Brumby, 41
Golan v. Saada, 109
Gonzales v. Carhart, 56, 69
Gonzales v. O Centro Espírita Beneficente União do Vegetal, 7
Gore v. Lee, 40
Grimm v. Gloucester Cty. School Bd., 40
Griswold v. Connecticut, 48, 57, 58, 60
Hecox v. Little, 40
Heller v. Doe, 55
High Plains Harvest Church v. Polis, 14
Hilton v. South Carolina Public Railways Comm'n, 68
Holloway v. Arthur Andersen & Co., 33
Hosanna-Tabor Evangelical Lutheran Church and School v. EEOC, 35
Human Embryo #4 HB-A By & Through Emma & Isabella Louisiana Tr. No. 1 v. Vergara, 89
Hurley v. Irish-American Gay, Lesbian and Bisexual Group of Boston, Inc., 13
Janus v. State, County, and Municipal Employees, 52
Johnson v. United States, 56
June Medical Services v. Russo, 52, 65
Kadel v. Folwell, 40
Kahler v. Kansas, 45
Kane v. Comm'r of Dep't of Health & Human Servs., 80
Karnoski v. Trump, 40
Keohane v. Florida Dept. of Corrections Secretary, 40
King v. Governor of the State of New Jersey, 95
Korematsu v. United States, 72
Kristen L. v. Benjamin W., 94
Lawrence v. Texas, 48, 57, 60
Lehnert v. Ferris Faculty Assn., 52
Lexmark Int'l, Inc. v. Static Control Components, Inc., 93
Loeb v. Vergara, 89
Los Angeles Dept. of Water and Power v. Manhart, 28
Loving v. Virginia, 17, 48, 58
Lozano v. Montoya Alvarez, 100, 114, 117
Madsen v. Women's Health Center, Inc., 53

Manahoy Area School District v.
    B.L., 75
Martin v. Franklin Capital Corp., 114
Masterpiece Cakeshop, Ltd. v.
    Colorado Civil Rights Comm'n, 3,
    12, 15
McDonald v. Chicago, 44, 57
McKown, People v., 91
Meyer v. Nebraska, 48
Michael I, In re, 81
Milner v. Department of Navy, 32
Monasky v. Taglieri, 99, 109
Moore v. East Cleveland, 48
Morton v. Mancari, 83, 84
NASA v. Nelson, 5
New Jersey Div. of Child Prot. &
    Permanency v. K.N.S., 81
Obergefell v. Hodges, 48, 57, 58, 60
Oncale v. Sundowner Offshore
    Services, Inc., 28
Parker, Commonwealth v., 46
Paul E. v. Courtney F., 94
Payne v. Tennessee, 49, 72
Pearson v. Callahan, 49
Pension Benefit Guaranty
    Corporation v. LTV Corp., 30
Phillips v. Martin Marietta Corp., 28
Pickup v. Brown, 95
Planned Parenthood of Southeastern
    Pa. v. Casey, 43, 52, 58, 59
Porter v. Ark. Dep't. of Health &
    Hum. Servs., 19
Price Waterhouse v. Hopkins, 27
Prince v. Massachusetts, 81
Proprietary v. Mitchell, 46
Ramos v. Louisiana, 52
Redmond v. Redmond, 102
Rochin v. California, 48
Roe v. Wade, 43, 57, 58, 60
Rogers v. Va. State Registrar, 17
Roman Catholic Diocese of Brooklyn
    v. Cuomo, 14
Santa Clara Pueblo v. Martinez, 84
Schrader v. Spain, 94
Sedima, S.P.R.L. v. Imrex Co., 32
Sessions v. Morales-Santana, 40
Shehadi v. Northeastern Nat. Bank
    of Pa., 6
Sherbert v. Verner, 4
Skinner v. Oklahoma ex rel.
    Williamson, 48
Smith v. Gaffard, 46
Smith v. Liberty Mut. Ins. Co., 33
Smith v. State, 46
Sullivan v. Finkelstein, 30
Tandon v. Newsom, 14, 81
Thomas v. Review Bd. of Ind.
    Employment Security Div., 3
Thornburgh v. American College of
    Obstetricians and Gynecologists,
    47
Timbs v. Indiana, 44

Troxel v. Granville, 92
Turner v. Safley, 48
University of Tex. Southwestern
    Medical Center v. Nassar, 25
Vasquez v. Hillery, 53
Vergara v. Loeb, 90
Virginia, United States v., 40
Washington v. Glucksberg, 44
Washington v. Harper, 48
Watson v. Fort Worth Bank & Trust,
    26
Whitaker v. Kenosha Unified School
    Dist. No. 1 Bd. of Ed., 40
Whitehouse v. Illinois Central R. Co.,
    59
Whole Woman's Health v.
    Hellerstedt, 51
Williams v. Frymire, 94
Winston v. Lee, 48
Zarda v. Altitude Express, Inc., 28

UNIVERSITY CASEBOOK SERIES®

2022 SUPPLEMENT TO
FAMILY LAW

CASES AND MATERIALS

**UNABRIDGED AND CONCISE
SEVENTH EDITIONS**

CHAPTER 1

AN INTRODUCTION TO FAMILY LAW

B. STRUCTURING FAMILY LAW: SOME APPROACHES

3. CONSERVATIVE CRITIQUE

On page 58 of the Unabridged 7th edition, and of the Concise 7th edition, after the Note, add the following introduction and case:

―――――

A vital question that has already started to surface involves how the Supreme Court, with its three new justices nominated by then-President Donald Trump, may weigh in with decisions that will impact family law and family law rules. *Fulton v. City Philadelphia* is an early and significant family law decision by the current Supreme Court's membership. Taken along with its more recent family law decisions, including *Dobbs v. Jackson Women's Health Org.*, in Chapter 3, what lessons may be learned from *Fulton* about how the current Court will approach family law doctrines that have in many ways been trending in liberal individualist and egalitarian directions, as indicated, perhaps more recently and most famously, by *Obergefell v. Hodges, supra*? How far might the Court move in the direction of vindicating conservative religious and traditional moral views, values, ideals, and rights in ways that intersect with established family law patterns?

Fulton v. City of Philadelphia
Supreme Court of the United States, 2021.
593 U.S. ___, 141 S.Ct. 1868, 210 L.Ed.2d 137.

■ CHIEF JUSTICE ROBERTS delivered the opinion of the Court.

Catholic Social Services [("CSS")] is a foster care agency in Philadelphia. The City stopped referring children to CSS upon discovering that the agency would not certify same-sex couples to be foster parents due to its religious beliefs about marriage. The City will renew its foster care contract with CSS only if the agency agrees to certify same-sex couples. The question presented is whether the actions of Philadelphia violate the First Amendment.

I

. . .

The Philadelphia foster care system depends on cooperation between the City and private foster agencies like CSS. When children cannot remain in their homes, the City's Department of Human Services assumes custody of them. The Department enters standard annual contracts with private foster agencies to place some of those children with foster families.

The placement process begins with review of prospective foster families. Pennsylvania law gives the authority to certify foster families to state-licensed foster agencies like CSS. 55 Pa. Code § 3700.61 (2020). Before certifying a family, an agency must conduct a home study during which it considers statutory criteria including the family's "ability to provide care, nurturing and supervision to children," "[e]xisting family relationships," and ability "to work in partnership" with a foster agency. § 3700.64. The agency must decide whether to "approve, disapprove or provisionally approve the foster family." § 3700.69.

When the Department seeks to place a child with a foster family, it sends its contracted agencies a request, known as a referral. The agencies report whether any of their certified families are available, and the Department places the child with what it regards as the most suitable family. The agency continues to support the family throughout the placement.

The religious views of CSS inform its work in this system. CSS believes that "marriage is a sacred bond between a man and a woman." Because the agency understands the certification of prospective foster families to be an endorsement of their relationships, it will not certify unmarried couples—regardless of their sexual orientation—or same-sex married couples. CSS does not object to certifying gay or lesbian individuals as single foster parents or to placing gay and lesbian children. No same-sex couple has ever sought certification from CSS. If one did, CSS would direct the couple to one of the more than 20 other agencies in the City, all of which currently certify same-sex couples. For over 50 years, CSS successfully contracted with the City to provide foster care services while holding to these beliefs. But things changed in 2018. After receiving a complaint about a different agency, a newspaper ran a story in which a spokesman for the Archdiocese of Philadelphia stated that CSS would not be able to consider prospective foster parents in same-sex marriages. The City Council called for an investigation, saying that the City had "laws in place to protect its people from discrimination that occurs under the guise of religious freedom." The Philadelphia Commission on Human Relations launched an inquiry. And the Commissioner of the Department of Human Services held a meeting with the leadership of CSS. She remarked that "things have changed since 100 years ago," and "it would be great if we followed the teachings of Pope Francis, the voice of the Catholic Church."

Immediately after the meeting, the Department informed CSS that it would no longer refer children to the agency. The City later explained that the refusal of CSS to certify same-sex couples violated a non-discrimination provision in its contract with the City as well as the non-discrimination requirements of the citywide Fair Practices Ordinance. The City stated that it would not enter a full foster care contract with CSS in the future unless the agency agreed to certify same-sex couples.

CSS and three foster parents affiliated with the agency filed suit against the City, the Department, and the Commission. The Support Center for Child Advocates and Philadelphia Family Pride intervened as defendants. As relevant here, CSS alleged that the referral freeze violated the Free Exercise and Free Speech Clauses of the First Amendment. CSS sought a temporary restraining order and preliminary injunction directing the Department to continue referring children to CSS without requiring the agency to certify same-sex couples.

. . .

II

A

The Free Exercise Clause of the First Amendment, applicable to the States under the Fourteenth Amendment, provides that "Congress shall make no law . . . prohibiting the free exercise" of religion. As an initial matter, it is plain that the City's actions have burdened CSS's religious exercise by putting it to the choice of curtailing its mission or approving relationships inconsistent with its beliefs. The City disagrees. In its view, certification reflects only that foster parents satisfy the statutory criteria, not that the agency endorses their relationships. But CSS believes that certification is tantamount to endorsement. And "religious beliefs need not be acceptable, logical, consistent, or comprehensible to others in order to merit First Amendment protection." *Thomas v. Review Bd. of Ind. Employment Security Div.*, 450 U.S. 707, 714 (1981). Our task is to decide whether the burden the City has placed on the religious exercise of CSS is constitutionally permissible. *Smith* held that laws incidentally burdening religion are ordinarily not subject to strict scrutiny under the Free Exercise Clause so long as they are neutral and generally applicable. 494 U.S., at 878–882. CSS urges us to overrule *Smith*[.] . . . But we need not revisit that decision here. This case falls outside *Smith* because the City has burdened the religious exercise of CSS through policies that do not meet the requirement of being neutral and generally applicable. See *Church of Lukumi Babalu Aye, Inc. v. Hialeah*, 508 U.S. 520, 531–532 (1993).

Government fails to act neutrally when it proceeds in a manner intolerant of religious beliefs or restricts practices because of their religious nature. See *Masterpiece Cakeshop, Ltd. v. Colorado Civil Rights Comm'n*, 584 U.S. ___, ___–___ (2018) (slip op., at 16–17); *Lukumi*, 508 U.S., at 533. CSS points to evidence in the record that it believes demonstrates that the City has transgressed this neutrality standard, but we find it more straightforward to resolve this case under the rubric of general applicability. A law is not generally applicable if it "invite[s]" the government to consider the particular reasons for a person's conduct by providing " 'a mechanism for individualized exemptions.' " *Smith*, 494 U.S., at 884. For example, in *Sherbert v. Verner*, 374 U.S. 398 (1963), a Seventh-day Adventist was fired because she would not work on Saturdays. Unable to find a job that would allow her to keep the Sabbath as her faith required, she applied for unemployment benefits. *Id.*, at 399–400. The State denied her application under a law prohibiting eligibility to claimants who had "failed, without good cause . . . to accept available suitable work." *Id.*, at 401 (internal quotation marks omitted). We held that the denial infringed her free exercise rights and could be justified only by a compelling interest. *Id.*, at 406.

Smith later explained that the unemployment benefits law in *Sherbert* was not generally applicable because the "good cause" standard permitted the government to grant exemptions based on the circumstances underlying each application. See 494 U.S., at 884. *Smith* went on to hold that "where the State has in place a system of individual exemptions, it may not refuse to extend that system to cases of 'religious hardship' without compelling reason." 494 U.S., at 884.

A law also lacks general applicability if it prohibits religious conduct while permitting secular conduct that undermines the government's asserted interests in a similar way. See *id.*, at 542–546. In *Church of Lukumi Babalu Aye, Inc. v. Hialeah*, for instance, the City of Hialeah adopted several ordinances prohibiting animal sacrifice, a practice of the Santeria faith. *Id.*, at 524–528. The City claimed that the ordinances were necessary in part to protect public health, which was "threatened by the disposal of animal carcasses in open public places." *Id.*, at 544. But the ordinances did not regulate hunters' disposal of their kills or improper garbage disposal by restaurants, both of which posed a similar hazard. *Id.*, at 544–545. The Court concluded that this and other forms of underinclusiveness meant that the ordinances were not generally applicable. *Id.*, at 545–546.

B

The City initially argued that CSS's practice violated section 3.21 of its standard foster care contract. We conclude, however, that this provision is not generally applicable as required by *Smith*. The current version of section 3.21 specifies in pertinent part:

> "**Rejection of Referral**. Provider shall not reject a child or family including, but not limited to, . . . prospective foster or adoptive parents, for Services based upon . . . their . . . sexual orientation . . . unless an exception is granted by the Commissioner or the Commissioner's designee, in his/her sole discretion."

This provision requires an agency to provide "Services," defined as "the work to be performed under this Contract," to prospective foster parents regardless of their sexual orientation.

Like the good cause provision in *Sherbert*, section 3.21 incorporates a system of individual exemptions, made available in this case at the "sole discretion" of the Commissioner. The City has made clear that the Commissioner "has no intention of granting an exception" to CSS. App. to Pet. for Cert. 168a. But the City "may not refuse to extend that [exemption] system to cases of 'religious hardship' without compelling reason." *Smith*, 494 U.S., at 884.

The City and intervenor-respondents resist this conclusion on several grounds. They first argue that governments should enjoy greater leeway under the Free Exercise Clause when setting rules for contractors than when regulating the general public. The government, they observe, commands heightened powers when managing its internal operations. See *NASA v. Nelson*, 562 U.S. 134, 150 (2011); *Engquist v. Oregon Dept. of Agriculture*, 553 U.S. 591, 598–600 (2008). And when individuals enter into government employment or contracts, they accept certain restrictions on their freedom as part of the deal. See *Garcetti v. Ceballos*, 547 U.S. 410, 418–420 (2006); *Board of Comm'rs, Wabaunsee Cty. v. Umbehr*, 518 U.S. 668, 677–678 (1996). Given this context, the City and intervenor-respondents contend, the government should have a freer hand when dealing with contractors like CSS.

These considerations cannot save the City here. As Philadelphia rightly acknowledges, "principles of neutrality and general applicability still constrain the government in its capacity as manager." We have never suggested that the government may discriminate against religion when acting in its managerial role. And *Smith* itself drew support for the neutral and generally applicable standard from cases involving internal government affairs. See 494 U.S., at 883–885, and n. 2. The City and intervenor-respondents accordingly ask only that courts apply a more deferential approach in determining whether a policy is neutral and generally applicable in the contracting context. We find no need to resolve that narrow issue in this case. No matter the level of deference we extend to the City, the inclusion of a formal system of entirely discretionary exceptions in section 3.21 renders the contractual nondiscrimination requirement not generally applicable. Perhaps all this explains why the City now contends that section 3.21 does not apply to CSS's refusal to certify same-sex couples after all. Instead, the City says that section 3.21 addresses only "an agency's right to refuse 'referrals' to place a child with a certified foster family." Brief for City Respondents 36. We think the City had it right the first time. Although the section is titled "Rejection of Referral," the text sweeps more broadly, forbidding the rejection of "prospective foster . . . parents" for "Services," without limitation. The City maintains that certification is one of the services foster agencies are hired to perform, so its attempt to backtrack on the reach of section 3.21 is unavailing. Moreover, the City adopted the current version of section 3.21 shortly after declaring that it would make CSS's obligation to certify same-sex couples "explicit" in future contracts, App. to Pet. for Cert. 170a, confirming our understanding of the text of the provision.

The City and intervenor-respondents add that, notwithstanding the system of exceptions in section 3.21, a separate provision in the contract independently prohibits discrimination in the certification of foster parents. That provision, section 15.1, bars discrimination on the basis of sexual orientation, and it does not on its face allow for exceptions. But state law makes clear that "one part of a contract cannot be so interpreted as to annul another part." *Shehadi v. Northeastern Nat. Bank of Pa.*, 474 Pa. 232, 236, 378 A. 2d 304, 306 (1977). Applying that "fundamental" rule here, an exception from section 3.21 also must govern the prohibition in section 15.1, lest the City's reservation of the authority to grant such an exception be a nullity. As a result, the contract as a whole contains no generally applicable non-discrimination requirement.

Finally, the City and intervenor-respondents contend that the availability of exceptions under section 3.21 is irrelevant because the Commissioner has never granted one. That misapprehends the issue. The creation of a formal mechanism for granting exceptions renders a policy not generally applicable, regardless whether any exceptions have been given, because it "invite[s]" the government to decide which reasons for not complying with the policy are worthy of solicitude, *Smith*, 494 U.S., at 884—here, at the Commissioner's "sole discretion."

. . .

C

In addition to relying on the contract, the City argues that CSS's refusal to certify same-sex couples constitutes an "Unlawful Public Accommodations Practice[ ]" in violation of the Fair Practices Ordinance. That ordinance forbids "deny[ing] or interfer[ing] with the public accommodations opportunities of an individual or otherwise discriminat[ing] based on his or her race, ethnicity, color, sex, sexual orientation, . . . disability, marital status, familial status," or several other protected categories. Phila. Code § 9–1106(1) (2016). The City contends that foster care agencies are public accommodations and therefore forbidden from discriminating on the basis of sexual orientation when certifying foster parents.

CSS counters that "foster care has never been treated as a 'public accommodation' in Philadelphia." In any event, CSS adds, the ordinance cannot qualify as generally applicable because the City allows exceptions to it for secular reasons despite denying one for CSS's religious exercise. But that constitutional issue arises only if the ordinance applies to CSS in the first place. We conclude that it does not because foster care agencies do not act as public accommodations in performing certifications.

. . .

The City asks us to adhere to the District Court's contrary determination that CSS qualifies as a public accommodation under the ordinance. The concurrence adopts the City's argument, seeing no incongruity in deeming a private religious foster agency a public accommodation. See *post*, at 3 (opinion of GORSUCH, J.). We respectfully disagree with the view of the City and the concurrence. . . . We agree with CSS's position, which it has maintained from the beginning of this dispute, that its "foster services do not constitute a 'public accommodation' under the City's Fair Practices Ordinance, and therefore it is not bound by that ordinance." We therefore have no need to assess whether the ordinance is generally applicable.

III

The contractual non-discrimination requirement imposes a burden on CSS's religious exercise and does not qualify as generally applicable. The concurrence protests that the "Court granted certiorari to decide whether to overrule [*Smith*]," and chides the Court for seeking to "sidestep the question." *Post*, at 1 (opinion of GORSUCH, J.). But the Court also granted review to decide whether Philadelphia's actions were permissible under our precedents. . . . CSS has demonstrated that the City's actions are subject to "the most rigorous of scrutiny" under those precedents. *Lukumi*, 508 U.S., at 546. Because the City's actions are therefore examined under the strictest scrutiny regardless of *Smith*, we have no occasion to reconsider that decision here.

A government policy can survive strict scrutiny only if it advances "interests of the highest order" and is narrowly tailored to achieve those interests. *Lukumi*, 508 U.S., at 546 (internal quotation marks omitted). Put another way, so long as the government can achieve its interests in a manner that does not burden religion, it must do so. The City asserts that its non-discrimination policies serve three compelling interests: maximizing the number of foster parents, protecting the City from liability, and ensuring equal treatment of prospective foster parents and foster children. The City states these objectives at a high level of generality, but the First Amendment demands a more precise analysis. See *Gonzales v. O Centro Espírita Beneficente União do Vegetal*, 546 U.S. 418, 430–432 (2006)[.] Rather than rely on "broadly formulated interests," courts must "scrutinize[ ] the asserted harm of granting specific exemptions to particular religious claimants." *O Centro*, 546 U.S., at 431. The question, then, is not whether the City has a compelling interest in enforcing its non-discrimination policies generally, but whether it has such an interest in denying an exception to CSS.

Once properly narrowed, the City's asserted interests are insufficient. Maximizing the number of foster families and minimizing liability are important goals, but the City fails to show that granting CSS an exception will put those goals at risk. If anything, including CSS in the program seems likely to increase, not reduce, the number of available foster parents. As for liability, the City offers only speculation that it might be sued over CSS's certification practices. Such speculation is insufficient to satisfy strict scrutiny ... particularly because the authority to certify foster families is delegated to agencies by the State, not the City, see 55 Pa. Code § 3700.61.

That leaves the interest of the City in the equal treatment of prospective foster parents and foster children. We do not doubt that this interest is a weighty one, for "[o]ur society has come to the recognition that gay persons and gay couples cannot be treated as social outcasts or as inferior in dignity and worth." *Masterpiece Cakeshop*, 584 U.S., at ___ (slip op., at 9). On the facts of this case, however, this interest cannot justify denying CSS an exception for its religious exercise. The creation of a system of exceptions under the contract undermines the City's contention that its nondiscrimination policies can brook no departures. See *Lukumi*, 508 U.S., at 546–547. The City offers no compelling reason why it has a particular interest in denying an exception to CSS while making them available to others.

* * *

As Philadelphia acknowledges, CSS has "long been a point of light in the City's foster-care system." Brief for City Respondents 1. CSS seeks only an accommodation that will allow it to continue serving the children of Philadelphia in a manner consistent with its religious beliefs; it does not seek to impose those beliefs on anyone else. The refusal of Philadelphia to contract with CSS for the provision of foster care services unless it agrees to certify same-sex couples as foster parents cannot survive strict scrutiny, and violates the First Amendment.

In view of our conclusion that the actions of the City violate the Free Exercise Clause, we need not consider whether they also violate the Free Speech Clause.

The judgment of the United States Court of Appeals for the Third Circuit is reversed, and the case is remanded for further proceedings consistent with this opinion.

It is so ordered.

■ JUSTICE BARRETT, with whom JUSTICE KAVANAUGH joins, and with whom JUSTICE BREYER joins as to all but the first paragraph, concurring.

In *Employment Div., Dept. of Human Resources of Ore. v. Smith*, 494 U.S. 872 (1990), this Court held that a neutral and generally applicable law typically does not violate the Free Exercise Clause—no matter how severely that law burdens religious exercise. Petitioners, their *amici*, scholars, and Justices of this Court have made serious arguments that *Smith* ought to be overruled. . . .

Yet what should replace *Smith*? The prevailing assumption seems to be that strict scrutiny would apply whenever a neutral and generally applicable law burdens religious exercise. But I am skeptical about swapping *Smith*'s categorical antidiscrimination approach for an equally categorical strict scrutiny regime, particularly when this Court's resolution of conflicts between generally applicable laws and other First Amendment rights—like speech and assembly—has been much more nuanced. There would be a number of issues to work through if *Smith* were overruled. To name a few: Should entities like Catholic Social Services—which is an arm of the Catholic Church—be treated differently than individuals? Should there be a distinction between indirect and direct burdens on religious exercise? And if the answer is strict scrutiny, would pre-*Smith* cases rejecting free exercise challenges to garden-variety laws come out the same way? See *Smith*, 494 U.S., at 888–889.

We need not wrestle with these questions in this case, though, because the same standard applies regardless whether *Smith* stays or goes. A longstanding tenet of our free exercise jurisprudence—one that both pre-dates and survives *Smith*—is that a law burdening religious exercise must satisfy strict scrutiny if it gives government officials discretion to grant individualized exemptions. See *id.*, at 884 . . . . As the Court's opinion today explains, the government contract at issue provides for individualized exemptions from its nondiscrimination rule, thus triggering strict scrutiny. And all nine Justices agree that the City cannot satisfy strict scrutiny. I therefore see no reason to decide in this case whether *Smith* should be overruled, much less what should replace it. I join the Court's opinion in full.

■ JUSTICE ALITO, with whom JUSTICE THOMAS and JUSTICE GORSUCH join, concurring in the judgment.

This case presents an important constitutional question that urgently calls out for review: whether this Court's governing interpretation of a bedrock constitutional right, the right to the free exercise of religion, is fundamentally wrong and should be corrected.

. . . *Employment Div., Dept. of Human Resources of Ore. v. Smith*, 494 U.S. 872 (1990), . . . [holding] that the First Amendment's Free Exercise Clause tolerates any rule that categorically prohibits or commands specified conduct so long as it does not target religious practice[,] . . . is ripe for reexamination.

I

. . .

. . . [T]he present case shows that the dangers posed by *Smith* are not hypothetical. The city of Philadelphia (City) has issued an ultimatum to an arm of the Catholic Church: Either engage in conduct that the Church views as contrary to the traditional Christian understanding of marriage or abandon a mission that dates back to the earliest days of the Church—providing for the care of orphaned and abandoned children. Many people believe they have a religious obligation to assist such children. Jews and Christians regard this as a scriptural command . . . and it is a mission that the Catholic Church has undertaken since ancient times. . . .

. . .

Whether with or without government participation, Catholic foster care agencies in Philadelphia and other cities have a long record of finding homes for children whose parents are unable or unwilling to care for them. Over the years, they have helped thousands of foster children and parents, and they take special pride in finding homes for children who are hard to place, including older children and those with special needs.

Recently, however, the City has barred Catholic Social Services (CSS) from continuing this work. Because the Catholic Church continues to believe that marriage is a bond between one man and one woman, CSS will not vet same-sex couples. As far as the record reflects, no same-sex couple has ever approached CSS, but if that were to occur, CSS would simply refer the couple to another agency that is happy to provide that service—and there are at least 27 such agencies in Philadelphia. . . . Thus, not only is there no evidence that CSS's policy has ever interfered in the slightest with the efforts of a same-sex couple to care for a foster child, there is no reason to fear that it would ever have that effect.

None of that mattered to Philadelphia. . . . [T]he City barred CSS from continuing its foster care work. Remarkably, the City took this step even though it threatens the welfare of children awaiting placement in foster homes. There is an acute shortage of foster parents, both in Philadelphia and in the country at large. . . . By ousting CSS, the City eliminated one of its major sources of foster homes. And that's not all. The City went so far as to prohibit the placement of any children in homes that CSS had previously vetted and approved. . . . The City apparently prefers to risk leaving children without foster parents than to allow CSS to follow its religiously dictated policy, which threatens no tangible harm. CSS broadly implies that the fundamental objective of City officials is to force the Philadelphia Archdiocese to change its position on marriage. Among other things, they point to statements by a City official deriding the Archdiocese's position as out of step with Pope Francis's teaching and 21st century moral views. . . . But whether or not this is the City's real objective, there can be no doubt that Philadelphia's ultimatum restricts CSS's ability to do what it believes the Catholic faith requires.

Philadelphia argues that its stance is allowed by *Smith*[.] . . . One of the questions that we accepted for review is "[w]hether *Employment Division v. Smith* should be revisited." We should confront that question.

Regrettably, the Court declines to do so. . . .

[The majority's] . . . decision might as well be written on the dissolving paper sold in magic shops. The City has been adamant about pressuring CSS to give in, and if the City wants to get around today's decision, it can simply eliminate the never-used exemption power. If it does that, then, voilà, today's decision will vanish—and the parties will be back where they started. The City will claim that it is protected by

Smith; CSS will argue that *Smith* should be overruled; the lower courts, bound by *Smith,* will reject that argument; and CSS will file a new petition in this Court challenging *Smith.* What is the point of going around in this circle? Not only is the Court's decision unlikely to resolve the present dispute, it provides no guidance regarding similar controversies in other jurisdictions. From 2006 to 2011, Catholic Charities in Boston, San Francisco, Washington, D. C., and Illinois ceased providing adoption or foster care services after the city or state government insisted that they serve same-sex couples. Although the precise legal grounds for these actions are not always clear, it appears that they were based on laws or regulations generally prohibiting discrimination on the basis of sexual orientation. And some jurisdictions have adopted anti-discrimination rules that expressly target adoption services.[23] Today's decision will be of no help in other cases involving the exclusion of faith-based foster care and adoption agencies unless by some chance the relevant laws contain the same glitch as the Philadelphia contractual provision on which the majority's decision hangs. The decision will be even less significant in all the other important religious liberty cases that are bubbling up.

We should reconsider *Smith* without further delay. . . .

. . .

III

A

That project must begin with the constitutional text. . . .

. . .

B

. . . [W]e should begin by considering the "normal and ordinary" meaning of the text of the Free Exercise Clause: "Congress shall make no law . . . prohibiting the free exercise [of religion]." Most of these terms and phrases—"Congress," "shall make," "no law," and "religion"—do not require discussion for present purposes, and we can therefore focus on what remains: the term "prohibiting" and the phrase "the free exercise of religion." Those words had essentially the same meaning in 1791 as they do today. "To prohibit" meant either "[t]o forbid" or "to hinder." 2 S. Johnson, A Dictionary of the English Language (1755) (Johnson (1755)). The term "exercise" had both a broad primary definition ("[p]ractice" or

---

[23] See, *e.g.,* Cal. Welf. & Inst. Code Ann. § 16013(a) (West 2018) (declaring that "all persons engaged in providing care and services to foster children, including . . . foster parents [and] adoptive parents . . . shall have fair and equal access to all available programs, services, benefits, and licensing processes, and shall not be subjected to discrimination . . . on the basis of . . . sexual orientation"); D. C. Munic. Regs., tit. 29, § 6003.1(d) (2018) (providing that foster parents are "[t]o not be subject to discrimination as provided in the D. C. Human Rights Act," which prohibits discrimination on the basis of sexual orientation); see also 110 Code Mass. Regs. 1.09(1) (2008) ("No applicant for or recipient of Department [of Children and Families] services shall, on the ground of . . . sexual orientation . . . be excluded from participation in, be denied the benefits of, or otherwise be subjected to discrimination in connection with any service, program, or activity administered or provided by the Department").

"outward performance") and a narrower secondary one (an "[a]ct of divine worship whether publick or private"). *id.* And "free," in the sense relevant here, meant "unrestrained." 1 Johnson (1755).

If we put these definitions together, the ordinary meaning of "prohibiting the free exercise of religion" was (and still is) forbidding or hindering unrestrained religious practices or worship. That straightforward understanding is a far cry from the interpretation adopted in *Smith.* It certainly does not suggest a distinction between laws that are generally applicable and laws that are targeted. . . .

The key point for present purposes is that the text of the Free Exercise Clause gives a specific group of people (those who wish to engage in the "exercise of religion") the right to do so without hindrance. . . .

. . .

. . . *Smith*'s interpretation conflicts with the ordinary meaning of the First Amendment's terms.

. . .

V

. . .

In assessing whether to overrule a past decision that appears to be incorrect, we have considered a variety of factors, and four of those weigh strongly against *Smith*: its reasoning; its consistency with other decisions; the workability of the rule that it established; and developments since the decision was handed down. See *Janus,* 585 U.S., at ___–___ (slip op., at 34–35). No relevant factor, including reliance, weighs in *Smith*'s favor.

A

Smith's reasoning. . . . *Smith* is a methodological outlier. It ignored the "normal and ordinary" meaning of the constitutional text . . . and it made no real effort to explore the understanding of the free-exercise right at the time of the First Amendment's adoption. . . .

Then there is *Smith*'s treatment of precedent. It looked for precedential support in strange places, and the many precedents that stood in its way received remarkably rough treatment. . . .

. . .

Smith's rough treatment of prior decisions diminishes its own status as a precedent.

B

Consistency with other precedents. Smith is also discordant with other precedents. . . .

. . .

There is . . . also tension between *Smith* and our opinion in *Masterpiece Cakeshop, Ltd. v. Colorado Civil Rights Comm'n,* 584 U.S.

___ (2018). In that case, we observed that "[w]hen it comes to weddings, it can be assumed that a member of the clergy who objects to gay marriage on moral and religious grounds could not be compelled to perform the ceremony without denial of his or her right to the free exercise of religion." *Id.*, at ___ (slip op., at 10). The clear import of this observation is that such a member of the clergy would be entitled to a religious exemption from a state law restricting the authority to perform a state-recognized marriage to individuals who are willing to officiate both opposite-sex and same-sex weddings.

Other inconsistencies exist. *Smith* declared that "a private right to ignore generally applicable laws" would be a "constitutional anomaly," 494 U.S., at 886, but this Court has often permitted exemptions from generally applicable laws in First Amendment cases. For instance, in *Boy Scouts of America v. Dale*, 530 U.S. 640, 656 (2000), we granted the Boy Scouts an exemption from an otherwise generally applicable state public accommodations law. In *Hurley v. Irish-American Gay, Lesbian and Bisexual Group of Boston, Inc.*, 515 U.S. 557, 573 (1995), parade sponsors' speech was exempted from the requirements of a similar law.

. . .

* * *

Multiple factors strongly favor overruling *Smith*. Are there countervailing factors?

E

None is apparent. . . .

. . .

For all these reasons, I would overrule *Smith* and reverse the decision below. Philadelphia's exclusion of CSS from foster care work violates the Free Exercise Clause, and CSS is therefore entitled to an injunction barring Philadelphia from taking such action.

. . .

■ JUSTICE GORSUCH, with whom JUSTICE THOMAS and JUSTICE ALITO join, concurring in the judgment.

. . .

. . . [T]he majority seems determined to declare there is no "need" or "reason" to revisit *Smith* today. . . .

But tell that to CSS. Its litigation has already lasted years—and today's (ir)resolution promises more of the same. Had we followed the path JUSTICE ALITO outlines—holding that the City's rules cannot avoid strict scrutiny even if they qualify as neutral and generally applicable— this case would end today. Instead, the majority's course guarantees that this litigation is only getting started. As the final arbiter of state law, the Pennsylvania Supreme Court can effectively overrule the majority's reading of the Commonwealth's public accommodations law. The City can revise its FPO to make even plainer still that its law does encompass foster services. Or with a flick of a pen, municipal lawyers may rewrite the City's contract to close the § 3.21 loophole.

Once any of that happens, CSS will find itself back where it started. The City has made clear that it will never tolerate CSS carrying out its foster-care mission in accordance with its sincerely held religious beliefs. To the City, it makes no difference that CSS has not denied service to a single same-sex couple; that dozens of other foster agencies stand willing to serve same-sex couples; or that CSS is committed to help any inquiring same-sex couples find those other agencies. The City has expressed its determination to put CSS to a choice: Give up your sincerely held religious beliefs or give up serving foster children and families. If CSS is unwilling to provide foster-care services to same-sex couples, the City prefers that CSS provide no foster-care services at all. This litigation thus promises to slog on for years to come, consuming time and resources in court that could be better spent serving children. And throughout it all, the opacity of the majority's professed endorsement of CSS's arguments ensures the parties will be forced to devote resources to the unenviable task of debating what it *even means*.

Nor will CSS bear the costs of the Court's indecision alone. Individuals and groups across the country will pay the price—in dollars, in time, and in continued uncertainty about their religious liberties. . . .

The costs of today's indecision fall on lower courts too. As recent cases involving COVID-19 regulations highlight, judges across the country continue to struggle to understand and apply *Smith*'s test even thirty years after it was announced. In the last nine months alone, this Court has had to intervene at least half a dozen times to clarify how *Smith* works. See, *e.g.,* [*Tandon v. Newsom,* 141 S.Ct. 1294 (2021) *(per curiam)*]; *Roman Catholic Diocese of Brooklyn v. Cuomo,* 592 U.S. ___ (2020) *(per curiam)*; *High Plains Harvest Church v. Polis,* 592 U.S. ___ (2020). . . . We owe it to the parties, to religious believers, and to our colleagues on the lower courts to cure the problem this Court created.

. . . *Smith* has been criticized since the day it was decided. No fewer than ten Justices—including six sitting Justices—have questioned its fidelity to the Constitution. The Court granted certiorari in this case to resolve its fate. . . . And not a single Justice has lifted a pen to defend the decision. So what are we waiting for?

. . .

NOTE

Fulton both resolves the dispute immediately involved in the case and maps out the prospects of a future Supreme Court decision overruling *Employment Division v. Smith.* If and when that happens, what might it mean for other family law rules? Some details, of course, are impossible to predict without knowing how the Court reasons its way to its conclusion in such a case. Still, it is not too soon to begin imagining the sorts of challenges grounded in First Amendment religious liberty claims that could arise in both a post-*Fulton* and a post-*Smith* world. More cases like *Masterpiece Cakeshop v. Colorado Civil Rights Commission*, 138 S.Ct. 1719 (2018), discussed in Chapter 2, involving challenges to public accommodations laws by religious business owners and their businesses wishing to refuse service to those whose ways of life are inconsistent with business owners' religious views and values are certainly coming down the pike. What other sorts of cases of religious freedom impacting family law rules can you see arising in *Fulton's* wake?

Viewed in a wider sense, *Fulton* is an indication of the current Supreme Court's receptiveness to, and even its solicitude for, conservative religious and traditional moral views, values, and claims of right in the context of constitutional decision-making. How might this approach shape the Court's treatment of other family law doctrines? Can you draw a line from *Fulton* to the Supreme Court's ruling in *Dobbs v. Jackson Women's Health Org.*, in Chapter 3. Does *Fulton* supply a useful background for thinking about what *Dobbs* may mean for LGBTQIA+ rights, including the right to marry? Do you see the Supreme Court beginning to define a new role for the Supreme Court in reshaping family law rules and thus how people in the United States shape their personal and intimate lives and relationships?

CHAPTER 2

MARRYING

B. RESTRICTIONS ON WHO MAY MARRY

1. CONSTITUTIONALITY OF MARRIAGE RESTRICTIONS

On page 76 of the Unabridged 7th edition (after note 6), and on page 67 of the Concise 7th edition (after note 3), add the following note:

In *Rogers v. Va. State Registrar*, 507 F.Supp.3d 664, 667, 670, 677 (E.D. Va. 2019), Judge Rossie D. Alston, Jr., struck down a Virginia law that required parties seeking a marriage license to "disclose their race in order to receive" the license as violative of the Due Process Clause of the Fourteenth Amendment. The Court's opinion traced "the historical underpinnings of the so called 'racial classification methodology' which cause[d] this case to be before [the] Court[,]" and characterized "the statutory scheme" at issue in the case as "a vestige of the nation's and of Virginia's history of codified racialization." *Id.* at 668–70. *See also id.* at 677. If *Rogers* is correct that this measure violates the Due Process Clause, because it impinges on the right to marry as announced in *Loving v. Virginia*, 388 U.S. 1, 12 (1967), *see Rogers, supra*, at 676–77, may the state properly require parties seeking a marriage license to disclose their birth sex or their gender identity? How might this impact the state's ability to track demographic data on marriages? Are there circumstances under which you might think it would be a good idea (or at least not a bad one) for a state to inquire about social identity markers from those who are seeking to marry?

2. TRADITIONAL RESTRICTIONS

b. AGE

On page 127 of the Unabridged 7th edition, and on page 104 of the Concise 7th edition, replace the notes with the following ones:

1. According to the lawyer for the father in the case: "On September 18, 2009[,] I presented to the trial Court an Order of Annulment which the Court granted. The Order set out that the Court of Appeals had made the finding [it did] . . . and that the Court needed to make an additional specific finding that the marriage should be and is annulled. The order was presented on Notice[,] but no one from the opposing sides showed up." E-mail from Ken Seaton to M. Spindelman, Professor of Law, Ohio State Univ. Moritz Coll. of Law (Sept. 22, 2011, 10:04 PDT) (on file with author).

2. At common law, children were considered capable of consenting to marriage at age seven, although the marriage was voidable by the underage party until he or she reached the "age of discretion," the presumptive age at

which the marriage could be consummated, which was twelve for girls and fourteen for boys.

Marriage by those who have not attained the age of majority is still widely permitted, including with parental consent or judicial override. *See* Amy Harmon & Alan Blinder, *Delaware Has Banned Marriage Under 18. Other States Also Consider Limits*, N.Y. TIMES (May 17, 2018), https://www.nytimes.com/2018/05/17/us/child-marriage-minimum-age-minors.html ("In the other 49 states, current law allows minors to marry, generally with parental consent or judicial approval."). A helpful state survey of marriage age requirements is available in NATIONAL SURVEY OF STATE LAWS 631–36 (Richard A. Leiter ed., 8th ed. 2019) (available as a HeinOnline database). In addition, statutory minimums may yield when certain exceptional circumstances exist, pregnancy being the most common. *See, e.g.*, ARK. CODE ANN. § 9–11–103 (West 2022).

3.   As a result of existing legal rules governing marriages by those who have not attained the age of majority, "underage" or "child marriages" are not at all uncommon. According to one analysis, "[m]ore than 207,000 people under 18 were married in the U.S. between 2000 and 2014[.] . . . While most minors were 16 or 17, some were as young as 12." Anjali Tsui, *Delaware Becomes First State to Ban Child Marriage*, PBS.ORG (May 9, 2018), https://www.pbs.org/wgbh/frontline/article/delaware-becomes-first-state-to-ban-child-marriage/.

The legal rules permitting these marriages are coming under increasing pressure across the country. Legal developments in Delaware are of especial note. *See* DEL. CODE ANN. tit. 13, § 123(a) (West 2022). "In Delaware, some 200 minors were married between 2000 and 2011, according to state health data. The majority—90 percent—were girls." Tsui, *supra*. In June 2018, Delaware changed its marriage age to 18, making it "the [first] . . . state where minors are unequivocally prevented from marrying before their 18th birthday." *Id.* Since then, legislation has been introduced in a number of jurisdictions to raise the marriage age. Is an exceptionless rule like Delaware's, limiting marriages to only those over 18 years of age, a good idea? What are its strongest justifications? *See, e.g.*, Nicholas Kristof, *An American 13-Year-Old, Pregnant and Married to Her Rapist*, N.Y. TIMES (June 1, 2018), https://www.nytimes.com/2018/06/01/opinion/sunday/child-marriage-delaware.html. Are the justifications that may be advanced in defense of an exceptionless rule like Delaware's an adequate legal warrant should the measure be subjected to constitutional challenge? What if the purpose of a marriage involving a minor is in whole or in part to ensure that a pregnant minor does not have a child out of wedlock? What if the marriage is consistent with both the minor's wishes and with the minor's parents' judgement? What if the marriage is consistent with the religious and/or cultural beliefs and/or practices of the group or community in which the minor lives? For relevant additional discussion, see Sarah Mueller, *Delaware Expected to Be the First State to Ban Child Marriage Outright*, NPR (May 3, 2018, 8:35PM), https://www.npr.org/2018/05/03/608351312/delaware-expected-to-be-the-first-state-to-ban-child-marriage-outright. Other states have followed Delaware's lead in completely prohibiting marriages for minors. For some recent commentary, see Nicholas Kristof, *A 14-Year-Old Bride, Wed to Her Rapist, Playing on a Jungle Gym*, N.Y. TIMES (June 19, 2021), https://www.nytimes.com/2021/06/19/opinion/sunday/child-marriage-rape.html ("[F]ive states have completely barred marriages by people under 18: Delaware, Minnesota, New Jersey, Pennsylvania and . . . Rhode Island. New York has passed a similar bill that is awaiting the governor's signature.").

4. Prohibitions on marriages involving one or more parties who are minors are scarcely the only means of enforcing a general policy against them. Child neglect proceedings provide another way of doing so. *See Porter v. Ark. Dep't. of Health & Hum. Servs.*, 286 S.W.3d 686, 694 (Ark. 2008) (upholding sufficiency of evidence behind trial court's findings in an abuse and dependency-neglect case partly involving a 16-year-old daughter allowed to marry a 34-year-old man); *In Interest of Flynn*, 318 N.E.2d 105 (Ill. App. Ct. 1974) (couple found unfit parents after they "sold" their 12-year-old daughter into marriage with a relative stranger for $28,000). *See also* Loretta M. Kopelman, *The Forced Marriage of Minors*, 44 J.L. MED. & ETHICS 173, 179 (2016) (arguing that "[t]he forced marriage of minors is child abuse and consequently [individuals and organizations that "have duties to prevent or stop child abuse"] . . . also have duties to prevent or stop the forced marriages of minors. These obligations arise from more general duties to safeguard their rights and wellbeing.").

5. Is the divorce rate for teenage marriages relevant to either a policy debate about the legality of underage marriage or to an assessment of rules against it as a constitutional matter? Is it significant that divorce rates for teenage marriages are higher than for other marriages, and that they have been for some time? Between 2006 and 2010, the reported probability of divorce within the first five years for women married under the age of 20 was 30 percent, while for women married between 20 and 24 years of age it was 19 percent. The reported probability for divorce for all women aged 15–44 within the first five years of marriage was 20 percent. *See* Casey E. Copen, et al., *First Marriages in the United States: Data From the 2006–2010 National Survey of Family Growth*, 49 NAT'L HEALTH STAT. REP. 1, 16 (2012).

To combat the high divorce rate of youth-involved marriages, some states have rules involving requirements for some premarital counseling. *See* CAL. FAM. CODE § 304 (West 2022) (authorizing courts to order premarital counseling for all couples in which one of the parties is a minor); MONT. CODE ANN. § 40–1–213 (West 2021) (required marriage counseling); UTAH CODE ANN. § 30–1–9(3)(c) (West 2022) ("The judge or court commissioner shall require that both parties to the marriage complete premarital counseling, except the requirement for premarital counseling may be waived if premarital counseling is not reasonably available."). Should such barriers to marriage be encouraged? Are they constitutional? What if these counseling requirements violate the religious views of the minor or minors seeking marriage? Does your answer depend on who is doing the counseling or how much of it is required?

6. The domestic U.S. legal rules on underage marriage may be situated in an international context:

Combating child marriage has become a core strategy for reducing teen births worldwide. Until the 1960s, international laws concerning marriage only loosely aimed to address adolescent fertility. Since then, the rise of global mobilization around human rights has called attention to both the negative consequences of adolescent fertility on girls and the roots of the problem. Not only do an overwhelming majority of births among adolescents in developing countries occur within marriage, contraceptive use is also less common for young wives, and early pregnancies are more likely when girls marry younger. Thus, organizations like UNICEF and the World Health Organization (WHO) continually place minimum-age-of-marriage laws front and center in their efforts to curb teenage childbearing.

International actors first identified child marriage as a problem in the Hague Conference in 1904 and first addressed it in international law in the 1962 Convention on Consent to Marriage, Minimum Age for Marriage, and Registration of Marriages (the Marriage Convention). The Marriage Convention, which called on states to set a minimum age of marriage at 15 years or older, was motivated by concern for basic human rights, opposition to slavery, and a desire to spread "one of the basic institutions of Occidental civilization" to the rest of the world. . . . The Marriage Convention was also not widely ratified. Even among countries that did ratify the Convention, very few set the minimum age at 18 years—the current international standard.

Whereas the Marriage Convention always had some link to human rights . . ., the inclusion of a marriage provision in the 1979 Convention for the Elimination of All Forms of Discrimination Against Women (CEDAW) more clearly cast child marriage as a rights issue. According to CEDAW, the "betrothal and the marriage of a child shall have no legal effect, and all necessary action, including legislation, shall be taken to specify a minimum age for marriage and to make the registration of marriages in an official registry compulsory" (Article 16, Para. 2). In addition, CEDAW General Recommendation 21 called on countries to legislate 18 years as the minimum marriage age. CEDAW was adopted to recognize and promote women's rights, and it explicitly connected those goals to the requirements first set out in the Marriage Convention.

More recently, child marriage has become a child rights as well as a women's rights issue. For example, the 1990 African Charter on the Rights and Welfare of the Child urged states to prohibit child marriages through legislation establishing the minimum age of marriage at 18. Similarly, the 1989 United Nations Convention on the Rights of the Child (CRC) has been viewed as obligating states to adopt minimum-age-of-marriage laws. For example, by requiring states to register all births, the CRC provides a tool for states to identify under-age marriages even when there is no formal state record of the marriage. Furthermore, while marriage is not specifically mentioned in the CRC, the Committee on the Rights of the Child (CRC Committee) routinely refers in its reports to the necessity of setting 18 years as the minimum age of marriage. At the international level, the rights framework of CEDAW and the CRC has received broader support than the moral framework of the earlier Marriage Convention. Unlike the Marriage Convention, the CRC has been widely ratified.

Minzee Kim et al., *When Do Laws Matter? National Minimum-Age-of-Marriage Laws, Child Rights, and Adolescent Fertility, 1989–2007*, 47 L. & SOC'Y REV. 589, 590–92 (2013) (citations and footnote omitted). Speaking generally, should domestic U.S. rules on underage marriage be harmonized with declared international norms? If so, under what circumstances? How might such arguments play in state legislative debates?

CHAPTER 3

MARRIAGE: LEGAL VISIONS OF PRIVACY, EQUALITY, AND VIOLENCE

B. CHALLENGES TO THE TRADITIONAL MARRIAGE MODEL

1. ECONOMIC AND SOCIAL CHANGES

On page 190 of the Unabridged 7th edition, and on page 152 of the Concise 7th edition, add the following note:

4. A recent story in the *New York Times* has noted that "over the past decade, as more women of all social classes have prioritized education and career, delaying childbearing has become a broad pattern among American women almost everywhere." Sabrina Tavernise, *et al.*, *Why American Women Everywhere Are Delaying Motherhood*, N.Y. TIMES (June 16, 2021), https://www.nytimes.com/2021/06/16/us/declining-birthrate-motherhood.html. As the story continues, "[t]he result has been the slowest growth of the American population since the 1930s, and a profound change in American motherhood." *Id.* "Women under 30 have become much less likely to have children. Since 2007, the birthrate for women in their 20s has fallen by 28 percent, and the biggest recent declines have been among unmarried women." *Id.* The story indicates that "[t]he only age groups in which birthrates rose over that period were women in their 30s and 40s—but even those began to decline over the past three years." What effect do you think this will have on challenges to the traditional marriage model? How might these changes intersect with the impacts of the COVID-19 epidemic on working women? For some reflections, see, for example, Nicole Bateman & Martha Ross, *Why Has COVID-19 Been Especially Harmful for Working Women*, BROOKINGS (Oct. 2020), https://www.brookings.edu/essay/why-has-covid-19-been-especially-harmful-for-working-women/; Sandrine Lungumbu & Amelia Butterly, *Coronavirus and Gender: More Chores for Women Set Back Gains in Equality*, BBC NEWS (Nov. 26, 2020), https://www.bbc.com/news/world-55016842; and Usha Ranji, *et al.*, *Women, Work, and Family During COVID-19: Findings from the KFF Women's Health Survey*, KAISER FAMILY FOUNDATION (Mar. 22, 2021), https://www.kff.org/womens-health-policy/issue-brief/women-work-and-family-during-covid-19-findings-from-the-kff-womens-health-survey/.

2. LEGAL LIMITS ON SEX DISCRIMINATION

b. POSITIVE LAW LIMITS ON SEX DISCRIMINATION

i. *Title VII*

On page 218 of the Unabridged 7th edition, and on page 173 of the Concise 7th edition, substitute the following case for *Hively v. Ivy Tech Community College of Indiana* and the introduction to it:

Bostock v. Clayton County, Georgia

Supreme Court of the United States, 2020.

590 U.S. ___, 140 S.Ct. 1731, 207 L.Ed.2d 218.

■ JUSTICE GORSUCH delivered the opinion of the Court.

. . . [I]n Title VII [of the 1964 Civil Rights Act], Congress outlawed discrimination in the workplace on the basis of race, color, religion, sex, or national origin. Today, we must decide whether an employer can fire someone simply for being homosexual or transgender. The answer is clear. An employer who fires an individual for being homosexual or transgender fires that person for traits or actions it would not have questioned in members of a different sex. Sex plays a necessary and undisguisable role in the decision, exactly what Title VII forbids.

. . .

I

Few facts are needed to appreciate the legal question we face. Each of the three cases before us started the same way: An employer fired a long-time employee shortly after the employee revealed that he or she is homosexual or transgender—and allegedly for no reason other than the employee's homosexuality or transgender status.

Gerald Bostock worked for Clayton County, Georgia, as a child welfare advocate. Under his leadership, the county won national awards for its work. After a decade with the county, Mr. Bostock began participating in a gay recreational softball league. Not long after that, influential members of the community allegedly made disparaging comments about Mr. Bostock's sexual orientation and participation in the league. Soon, he was fired for conduct "unbecoming" a county employee.

Donald Zarda worked as a skydiving instructor at Altitude Express in New York. After several seasons with the company, Mr. Zarda mentioned that he was gay and, days later, was fired.

Aimee Stephens worked at R.G. & G.R. Harris Funeral Homes in Garden City, Michigan. When she got the job, Ms. Stephens presented as a male. But two years into her service with the company, she began treatment for despair and loneliness. Ultimately, clinicians diagnosed her with gender dysphoria and recommended that she begin living as a woman. In her sixth year with the company, Ms. Stephens wrote a letter to her employer explaining that she planned to "live and work full-time as a woman" after she returned from an upcoming vacation. The funeral home fired her before she left, telling her "this is not going to work out."

. . . During the course of the proceedings in these long-running disputes, both Mr. Zarda and Ms. Stephens have passed away. But their estates continue to press their causes for the benefit of their heirs. . . .

II

This Court normally interprets a statute in accord with the ordinary public meaning of its terms at the time of its enactment. After all, only the words on the page constitute the law adopted by Congress and approved by the President. . . .

With this in mind, our task is clear. We must determine the ordinary public meaning of Title VII's command that it is "unlawful . . . for an employer to fail or refuse to hire or to discharge any individual, or otherwise to discriminate against any individual with respect to his compensation, terms, conditions, or privileges of employment, because of such individual's race, color, religion, sex, or national origin." [42 U.S.C.] § 2000e–2(a)(1). To do so, we orient ourselves to the time of the statute's adoption, here 1964, and begin by examining the key statutory terms in turn before assessing their impact on the cases at hand and then confirming our work against this Court's precedents.

A

The only statutorily protected characteristic at issue in today's cases is "sex"—and that is also the primary term in Title VII whose meaning the parties dispute. Appealing to roughly contemporaneous dictionaries, the employers say that, as used here, the term "sex" in 1964 referred to "status as either male or female [as] determined by reproductive biology." . . . [B]ecause the employees concede the point for argument's sake, we proceed on the assumption that "sex" signified what the employers suggest, referring only to biological distinctions between male and female.

. . . The question isn't just what "sex" meant, but what Title VII says about it. Most notably, the statute prohibits employers from taking certain actions "because of" sex. . . . Title VII's "because of" test incorporates the " 'simple' " and "traditional" standard of but-for causation. [*University of Tex. Southwestern Medical Center v.*] *Nassar*, 570 U.S. [338,] 346, 360 [(2013)]. That form of causation is established whenever a particular outcome would not have happened "but for" the purported cause. In other words, a but-for test directs us to change one thing at a time and see if the outcome changes. If it does, we have found a but-for cause.

. . . So long as the plaintiff's sex was one but-for cause of that decision, that is enough to trigger the law.

. . .

As sweeping as even the but-for causation standard can be, Title VII does not concern itself with everything that happens "because of" sex. The statute imposes liability on employers only when they "fail or refuse to hire," "discharge," "or otherwise . . . discriminate against" someone because of a statutorily protected characteristic like sex. [§ 2000e–2(a)(1).] The employers acknowledge that they discharged the plaintiffs in today's cases, but assert that the statute's list of verbs is qualified by the last item on it: "otherwise . . . discriminate against." By virtue of the word *otherwise*, the employers suggest, Title VII concerns itself not with every discharge, only with those discharges that involve discrimination.

Accepting this point, too, for argument's sake, the question becomes: What did "discriminate" mean in 1964? As it turns out, it meant then roughly what it means today: "To make a difference in treatment or favor (of one as compared with others)." Webster's New International Dictionary 745 (2d ed. 1954). To "discriminate against" a person, then, would seem to mean treating that individual worse than others who are similarly situated. See *Burlington N. & S. F. R. Co. v. White*, 548 U.S. 53, 59 (2006). In so-called "disparate treatment" cases like today's, this Court has also held that the difference in treatment based on sex must be intentional. See, *e.g., Watson v. Fort Worth Bank & Trust*, 487 U.S. 977, 986 (1988). So, taken together, an employer who intentionally treats a person worse because of sex—such as by firing the person for actions or attributes it would tolerate in an individual of another sex—discriminates against that person in violation of Title VII.

. . .

The statute . . . tells us three times—including immediately after the words "discriminate against"—that our focus should be on individuals, not groups[.] . . . And the meaning of "individual" was as uncontroversial in 1964 as it is today: "A particular being as distinguished from a class, species, or collection." Webster's New International Dictionary, at 1267. . . .

The consequences of the law's focus on individuals rather than groups are anything but academic. Suppose an employer fires a woman for refusing his sexual advances. It's no defense for the employer to note that, while he treated that individual woman worse than he would have treated a man, he gives preferential treatment to female employees overall. The employer is liable for treating *this* woman worse in part because of her sex. Nor is it a defense for an employer to say it discriminates against both men and women because of sex. This statute works to protect individuals of both sexes from discrimination, and does so equally. So an employer who fires a woman, Hannah, because she is insufficiently feminine and also fires a man, Bob, for being insufficiently masculine may treat men and women as groups more or less equally. But in *both* cases the employer fires an individual in part because of sex. Instead of avoiding Title VII exposure, this employer doubles it.

B

From the ordinary public meaning of the statute's language at the time of the law's adoption, a straightforward rule emerges: An employer violates Title VII when it intentionally fires an individual employee based in part on sex. It doesn't matter if other factors besides the plaintiff's sex contributed to the decision. And it doesn't matter if the employer treated women as a group the same when compared to men as a group. If the employer intentionally relies in part on an individual employee's sex when deciding to discharge the employee—put differently, if changing the employee's sex would have yielded a different choice by the employer—a statutory violation has occurred. Title VII's message is "simple but momentous": An individual employee's sex is "not relevant to the selection, evaluation, or compensation of employees." *Price Waterhouse v. Hopkins*, 490 U.S. 228, 239 (1989) (plurality opinion).

The statute's message for our cases is equally simple and momentous: An individual's homosexuality or transgender status is not relevant to employment decisions. That's because it is impossible to discriminate against a person for being homosexual or transgender without discriminating against that individual based on sex. Consider, for example, an employer with two employees, both of whom are attracted to men. The two individuals are, to the employer's mind, materially identical in all respects, except that one is a man and the other a woman. If the employer fires the male employee for no reason other than the fact he is attracted to men, the employer discriminates against him for traits or actions it tolerates in his female colleague. Put differently, the employer intentionally singles out an employee to fire based in part on the employee's sex, and the affected employee's sex is a but-for cause of his discharge. Or take an employer who fires a transgender person who was identified as a male at birth but who now identifies as a female. If the employer retains an otherwise identical employee who was identified as female at birth, the employer intentionally penalizes a person identified as male at birth for traits or actions that it tolerates in an employee identified as female at birth. Again, the individual employee's sex plays an unmistakable and impermissible role in the discharge decision.

. . .

. . . [I]ntentional discrimination based on sex violates Title VII, even if it is intended only as a means to achieving the employer's ultimate goal of discriminating against homosexual or transgender employees. There is simply no escaping the role intent plays here: Just as sex is necessarily a but-for *cause* when an employer discriminates against homosexual or transgender employees, an employer who discriminates on these grounds inescapably *intends* to rely on sex in its decisionmaking. Imagine an employer who has a policy of firing any employee known to be homosexual. The employer hosts an office holiday party and invites employees to bring their spouses. A model employee arrives and introduces a manager to Susan, the employee's wife. Will that employee be fired? If the policy works as the employer intends, the answer depends entirely on whether the model employee is a man or a woman. To be sure, that employer's ultimate goal might be to discriminate on the basis of sexual orientation. But to achieve that purpose the employer must, along the way, intentionally treat an employee worse based in part on that individual's sex.

An employer musters no better a defense by responding that it is equally happy to fire male *and* female employees who are homosexual or transgender. Title VII liability is not limited to employers who, through the sum of all of their employment actions, treat the class of men differently than the class of women. Instead, the law makes each instance of discriminating against an individual employee because of that individual's sex an independent violation of Title VII. So just as an employer who fires both Hannah and Bob for failing to fulfill traditional sex stereotypes doubles rather than eliminates Title VII liability, an employer who fires both Hannah and Bob for being gay or transgender does the same.

At bottom, these cases involve no more than the straightforward application of legal terms with plain and settled meanings. For an employer to discriminate against employees for being homosexual or transgender, the employer must intentionally discriminate against individual men and women in part because of sex. That has always been prohibited by Title VII's plain terms—and that "should be the end of the analysis." [*Zarda v. Altitude Express, Inc.*,] 883 F.3d [100,] 135 [(2d Cir. 2018)] (Cabranes, J., concurring in judgment).

C

If more support for our conclusion were required, there's no need to look far. All that the statute's plain terms suggest, this Court's cases have already confirmed. . . . [See *Phillips v. Martin Marietta Corp.*, 400 U.S. 542 (1971) (*per curiam*); *Los Angeles Dept. of Water and Power v. Manhart*, 435 U.S. 702 (1978); *Oncale v. Sundowner Offshore Services, Inc.*, 523 U.S. 75 (1998).]

. . .

The lessons these cases hold for ours are by now familiar.

First, it's irrelevant what an employer might call its discriminatory practice, how others might label it, or what else might motivate it. . . .

Second, the plaintiff's sex need not be the sole or primary cause of the employer's adverse action. . . .

Finally, an employer cannot escape liability by demonstrating that it treats males and females comparably as groups. . . .

III

What do the employers have to say in reply? For present purposes, they do not dispute that they fired the plaintiffs for being homosexual or transgender. Sorting out the true reasons for an adverse employment decision is often a hard business, but none of that is at issue here. Rather, the employers submit that even intentional discrimination against employees based on their homosexuality or transgender status supplies no basis for liability under Title VII.

The employers' argument proceeds in two stages. Seeking footing in the statutory text, they begin by advancing a number of reasons why discrimination on the basis of homosexuality or transgender status doesn't involve discrimination because of sex. But each of these arguments turns out only to repackage errors we've already seen and this Court's precedents have already rejected. In the end, the employers are left to retreat beyond the statute's text, where they fault us for ignoring the legislature's purposes in enacting Title VII or certain expectations about its operation. They warn, too, about consequences that might follow a ruling for the employees. But none of these contentions about what the employers think the law was meant to do, or should do, allow us to ignore the law as it is.

A

Maybe most intuitively, the employers assert that discrimination on the basis of homosexuality and transgender status aren't referred to as sex discrimination in ordinary conversation. If asked by a friend (rather than a judge) why they were fired, even today's plaintiffs would likely respond that it was because they were gay or transgender, not because of sex. According to the employers, that conversational answer, not the statute's strict terms, should guide our thinking and suffice to defeat any suggestion that the employees now before us were fired because of sex.

But this submission rests on a mistaken understanding of what kind of cause the law is looking for in a Title VII case. In conversation, a speaker is likely to focus on what seems most relevant or informative to the listener. So an employee who has just been fired is likely to identify the primary or most direct cause rather than list literally every but-for cause. To do otherwise would be tiring at best. But these conversational conventions do not control Title VII's legal analysis, which asks simply whether sex was a but-for cause. . . . You can call the statute's but-for causation test what you will—expansive, legalistic, the dissents even dismiss it as wooden or literal. But it is the law.

Trying another angle, the defendants before us suggest that an employer who discriminates based on homosexuality or transgender status doesn't *intentionally* discriminate based on sex, as a disparate treatment claim requires. But, as we've seen, an employer who discriminates against homosexual or transgender employees necessarily and intentionally applies sex-based rules. An employer that announces it will not employ anyone who is homosexual, for example, intends to penalize male employees for being attracted to men and female employees for being attracted to women.

. . .

Next, the employers turn to Title VII's list of protected characteristics—race, color, religion, sex, and national origin. Because homosexuality and transgender status can't be found on that list and because they are conceptually distinct from sex, the employers reason, they are implicitly excluded from Title VII's reach. . . .

. . . We agree that homosexuality and transgender status are distinct concepts from sex. But, as we've seen, discrimination based on homosexuality or transgender status necessarily entails discrimination based on sex; the first cannot happen without the second. Nor is there any such thing as a "canon of donut holes," in which Congress's failure to speak directly to a specific case that falls within a more general statutory rule creates a tacit exception. Instead, when Congress chooses not to include any exceptions to a broad rule, courts apply the broad rule. And that is exactly how this Court has always approached Title VII. . . . As enacted, Title VII prohibits all forms of discrimination because of sex, however they may manifest themselves or whatever other labels might attach to them.

The employers try the same point another way. Since 1964, they observe, Congress has considered several proposals to add sexual orientation to Title VII's list of protected characteristics, but no such amendment has become law. Meanwhile, Congress has enacted other statutes addressing other topics that do discuss sexual orientation. This postenactment legislative history, they urge, should tell us something.

. . . [S]peculation about why a later Congress declined to adopt new legislation offers a "particularly dangerous" basis on which to rest an interpretation of an existing law a different and earlier Congress did adopt. *Pension Benefit Guaranty Corporation v. LTV Corp.*, 496 U.S. 633, 650 (1990); *Sullivan v. Finkelstein*, 496 U.S. 617, 632 (1990) (Scalia, J., concurring) ("Arguments based on subsequent legislative history . . . should not be taken seriously, not even in a footnote").

That leaves the employers to seek a different sort of exception. Maybe the traditional and simple but-for causation test should apply in all other Title VII cases, but it just doesn't work when it comes to cases involving homosexual and transgender employees. The test is too blunt to capture the nuances here. The employers illustrate their concern with an example. When we apply the simple test to Mr. Bostock—asking whether Mr. Bostock, a man attracted to other men, would have been fired had he been a woman—we don't just change his sex. Along the way, we change his sexual orientation too (from homosexual to heterosexual). If the aim is to isolate whether a plaintiff's sex caused the dismissal, the employers stress, we must hold sexual orientation constant—meaning we need to change both his sex and the sex to which he is attracted. So for Mr. Bostock, the question should be whether he would've been fired if he were a woman attracted to women. And because his employer would have been as quick to fire a lesbian as it was a gay man, the employers conclude, no Title VII violation has occurred.

While the explanation is new, the mistakes are the same. The employers might be onto something if Title VII only ensured equal treatment between groups of men and women or if the statute applied only when sex is the sole or primary reason for an employer's challenged adverse employment action. But both of these premises are mistaken. Title VII's plain terms and our precedents don't care if an employer treats men and women comparably as groups; an employer who fires both lesbians and gay men equally doesn't diminish but doubles its liability. . . .

Still, the employers insist, something seems different here. Unlike certain other employment policies this Court has addressed that harmed only women or only men, the employers' policies in the cases before us have the same adverse consequences for men and women. How could sex be necessary to the result if a member of the opposite sex might face the same outcome from the same policy?

What the employers see as unique isn't even unusual. Often in life and law two but-for factors combine to yield a result that could have also occurred in some other way. Imagine that it's a nice day outside and your house is too warm, so you decide to open the window. Both the cool temperature outside and the heat inside are but-for causes of your choice to open the window. That doesn't change just because you also would have opened the window had it been warm outside and cold inside. In either case, no one would deny that the window is open "because of" the outside temperature. Our cases are much the same. So, for example, when it comes to homosexual employees, male sex and attraction to men are but-for factors that can combine to get them fired. The fact that female sex and attraction to women can *also* get an employee fired does no more than show the same outcome can be achieved through the combination of different factors. In either case, though, sex plays an essential but-for role.

At bottom, the employers' argument unavoidably comes down to a suggestion that sex must be the sole or primary cause of an adverse employment action for Title VII liability to follow. And ... that suggestion is at odds with everything we know about the statute. Consider an employer eager to revive the workplace gender roles of the 1950s. He enforces a policy that he will hire only men as mechanics and only women as secretaries. When a qualified woman applies for a mechanic position and is denied, the "simple test" immediately spots the discrimination: A qualified man would have been given the job, so sex was a but-for cause of the employer's refusal to hire. But like the employers before us today, this employer would say not so fast. By comparing the woman who applied to be a mechanic to a man who applied to be a mechanic, we've quietly changed two things: the applicant's sex and her trait of failing to conform to 1950s gender roles. The "simple test" thus overlooks that it is really the applicant's bucking of 1950s gender roles, not her sex, doing the work. So we need to hold that second trait constant: Instead of comparing the disappointed female applicant to a man who applied for the same position, the employer would say, we should compare her to a man who applied to be a secretary. And because that jobseeker would be refused too, this must not be sex discrimination.

No one thinks *that*, so the employers must scramble to justify deploying a stricter causation test for use only in cases involving discrimination based on sexual orientation or transgender status. Such a rule would create a curious discontinuity in our case law, to put it mildly. Employer hires based on sexual stereotypes? Simple test. Employer sets pension contributions based on sex? Simple test. Employer fires men who do not behave in a sufficiently masculine way around the office? Simple test. But when that same employer discriminates against women who are attracted to women, or persons identified at birth as women who later identify as men, we suddenly roll out a new and more rigorous standard? Why are *these* reasons for taking sex into account different from all the rest? Title VII's text can offer no answer.

B

Ultimately, the employers are forced to abandon the statutory text and precedent altogether and appeal to assumptions and policy. Most pointedly, they contend that few in 1964 would have expected Title VII to apply to discrimination against homosexual and transgender persons. And whatever the text and our precedent indicate, they say, shouldn't this fact cause us to pause before recognizing liability?

It might be tempting to reject this argument out of hand. This Court has explained many times over many years that, when the meaning of the statute's terms is plain, our job is at an end. The people are entitled to rely on the law as written, without fearing that courts might disregard its plain terms based on some extratextual consideration. Of course, some Members of this Court have consulted legislative history when interpreting *ambiguous* statutory language. "Legislative history, for those who take it into account, is meant to clear up ambiguity, not create it." *Milner v. Department of Navy*, 562 U.S. 562, 574 (2011). And as we have seen, no ambiguity exists about how Title VII's terms apply to the facts before us. To be sure, the statute's application in these cases reaches "beyond the principal evil" legislators may have intended or expected to address. *Oncale*, 523 U.S. at 79. But " 'the fact that [a statute] has been applied in situations not expressly anticipated by Congress' " does not demonstrate ambiguity; instead, it simply " 'demonstrates [the] breadth' " of a legislative command. *Sedima, S.P.R.L. v. Imrex Co.*, 473 U.S. 479, 499 (1985). And "it is ultimately the provisions of" those legislative commands "rather than the principal concerns of our legislators by which we are governed." *Oncale*, 523 U.S. at 79; see also A. Scalia & B. Garner, Reading Law: The Interpretation of Legal Texts 101 (2012) (noting that unexpected applications of broad language reflect only Congress's "presumed point [to] produce general coverage—not to leave room for courts to recognize ad hoc exceptions").

. . .

. . . [T]he employers and dissents . . . suggest that, because few in 1964 expected today's *result*, we should not dare to admit that it follows ineluctably from the statutory text. When a new application emerges that is both unexpected and important, they would seemingly have us merely point out the question, refer the subject back to Congress, and decline to enforce the plain terms of the law in the meantime.

That is exactly the sort of reasoning this Court has long rejected. . . .

If anything, the employers' . . . framing may only add new problems. The employers assert that "no one" in 1964 or for some time after would have anticipated today's result. But is that really true? Not long after the law's passage, gay and transgender employees began filing Title VII complaints, so at least *some* people foresaw this potential application. See, *e.g.*, *Smith v. Liberty Mut. Ins. Co.*, 395 F.Supp. 1098, 1099 (ND Ga. 1975) (addressing claim from 1969); *Holloway v. Arthur Andersen & Co.*, 566 F.2d 659, 661 (CA9 1977) (addressing claim from 1974). And less than a decade after Title VII's passage, during debates over the Equal Rights Amendment, others counseled that its language—which was strikingly similar to Title VII's—might also protect homosexuals from discrimination. See, *e.g.*, Note, The Legality of Homosexual Marriage, 82 Yale L. J. 573, 583–584 (1973).

Why isn't that enough to demonstrate that today's result isn't totally unexpected? How many people have to foresee the application for it to qualify as "expected"? Do we look only at the moment the statute was enacted, or do we allow some time for the implications of a new statute to be worked out? Should we consider the expectations of those who had no reason to give a particular application any thought or only those with reason to think about the question? How do we account for those who change their minds over time, after learning new facts or hearing a new argument? How specifically or generally should we frame the "application" at issue? None of these questions have obvious answers, and the employers don't propose any.

One could also reasonably fear that objections about unexpected applications will not be deployed neutrally. Often lurking just behind such objections resides a cynicism that Congress could not *possibly* have meant to protect a disfavored group. . . . [A]pplying protective laws to groups that were politically unpopular at the time of the law's passage— whether prisoners in the 1990s or homosexual and transgender employees in the 1960s—often may be seen as unexpected. But to refuse enforcement just because of that, because the parties before us happened to be unpopular at the time of the law's passage, would not only require us to abandon our role as interpreters of statutes; it would tilt the scales of justice in favor of the strong or popular and neglect the promise that all persons are entitled to the benefit of the law's terms.

The employer's position also proves too much. If we applied Title VII's plain text only to applications some (yet-to-be-determined) group expected in 1964, we'd have more than a little law to overturn. . . .

. . .

With that, the employers are left to abandon their concern for expected applications and fall back to the last line of defense for all failing statutory interpretation arguments: naked policy appeals. If we were to apply the statute's plain language, they complain, any number of undesirable policy consequences would follow. Gone here is any pretense of statutory interpretation; all that's left is a suggestion we should proceed without the law's guidance to do as we think best. But that's an invitation no court should ever take up. The place to make new legislation, or address unwanted consequences of old legislation, lies in Congress. When it comes to statutory interpretation, our role is limited to applying the law's demands as faithfully as we can in the cases that come before us. As judges we possess no special expertise or authority to declare for ourselves what a self-governing people should consider just or wise. And the same judicial humility that requires us to refrain from adding to statutes requires us to refrain from diminishing them.

What are these consequences anyway? The employers worry that our decision will sweep beyond Title VII to other federal or state laws that prohibit sex discrimination. And, under Title VII itself, they say sex-segregated bathrooms, locker rooms, and dress codes will prove unsustainable after our decision today. But none of these other laws are before us; we have not had the benefit of adversarial testing about the meaning of their terms, and we do not prejudge any such question today. Under Title VII, too, we do not purport to address bathrooms, locker rooms, or anything else of the kind. The only question before us is whether an employer who fires someone simply for being homosexual or transgender has discharged or otherwise discriminated against that individual "because of such individual's sex." As used in Title VII, the term " 'discriminate against' " refers to "distinctions or differences in treatment that injure protected individuals." *Burlington N. & S.F.R.*, 548 U.S. at 59. Firing employees because of a statutorily protected trait surely counts. Whether other policies and practices might or might not qualify as unlawful discrimination or find justifications under other provisions of Title VII are questions for future cases, not these.

Separately, the employers fear that complying with Title VII's requirement in cases like ours may require some employers to violate their religious convictions. We are also deeply concerned with preserving the promise of the free exercise of religion enshrined in our Constitution; that guarantee lies at the heart of our pluralistic society. But worries about how Title VII may intersect with religious liberties are nothing new; they even predate the statute's passage. As a result of its deliberations in adopting the law, Congress included an express statutory exception for religious organizations. § 2000e–1(a). This Court has also recognized that the First Amendment can bar the application of employment discrimination laws "to claims concerning the employment relationship between a religious institution and its ministers." *Hosanna-Tabor Evangelical Lutheran Church and School v. EEOC*, 565 U.S. 171, 188 (2012). And Congress has gone a step further yet in the Religious Freedom Restoration Act of 1993 (RFRA), 107 Stat. 1488, codified at 42 U.S.C. § 2000bb *et seq.* That statute prohibits the federal government from substantially burdening a person's exercise of religion unless it demonstrates that doing so both furthers a compelling governmental interest and represents the least restrictive means of furthering that interest. § 2000bb–1. Because RFRA operates as a kind of super statute, displacing the normal operation of other federal laws, it might supersede Title VII's commands in appropriate cases. See § 2000bb–3.

But how these doctrines protecting religious liberty interact with Title VII are questions for future cases too. Harris Funeral Homes did unsuccessfully pursue a RFRA-based defense in the proceedings below. In its certiorari petition, however, the company declined to seek review of that adverse decision, and no other religious liberty claim is now before us. So while other employers in other cases may raise free exercise arguments that merit careful consideration, none of the employers before us today represent in this Court that compliance with Title VII will infringe their own religious liberties in any way.

*

. . .

. . . Ours is a society of written laws. Judges are not free to overlook plain statutory commands on the strength of nothing more than suppositions about intentions or guesswork about expectations. In Title VII, Congress adopted broad language making it illegal for an employer to rely on an employee's sex when deciding to fire that employee. We do not hesitate to recognize today a necessary consequence of that legislative choice: An employer who fires an individual merely for being gay or transgender defies the law.

. . .

■ JUSTICE ALITO, with whom JUSTICE THOMAS joins, dissenting.

There is only one word for what the Court has done today: legislation. . . .

Title VII of the Civil Rights Act of 1964 prohibits employment discrimination on any of five specified grounds: "race, color, religion, sex, [and] national origin." 42 U.S.C. § 2000e–2(a)(1). Neither "sexual orientation" nor "gender identity" appears on that list. For the past 45 years, bills have been introduced in Congress to add "sexual orientation" to the list, and in recent years, bills have included "gender identity" as well. But to date, none has passed both Houses.

Last year, the House of Representatives passed a bill that would amend Title VII by defining sex discrimination to include both "sexual orientation" and "gender identity," H.R. 5, 116th Cong., 1st Sess. (2019), but the bill has stalled in the Senate. An alternative bill, H.R. 5331, 116th Cong., 1st Sess. (2019), would add similar prohibitions but contains provisions to protect religious liberty. This bill remains before a House Subcommittee.

Because no such amendment of Title VII has been enacted in accordance with the requirements in the Constitution (passage in both Houses and presentment to the President, Art. I, § 7, cl. 2), Title VII's prohibition of discrimination because of "sex" still means what it has always meant. But the Court is not deterred by these constitutional niceties. Usurping the constitutional authority of the other branches, the Court has essentially taken H.R. 5's provision on employment discrimination and issued it under the guise of statutory interpretation.[4] A more brazen abuse of our authority to interpret statutes is hard to recall.

The Court tries to convince readers that it is merely enforcing the terms of the statute, but that is preposterous. Even as understood today, the concept of discrimination because of "sex" is different from discrimination because of "sexual orientation" or "gender identity." And in any event, our duty is to interpret statutory terms to "mean what they conveyed to reasonable people *at the time they were written.*" A. Scalia & B. Garner, Reading Law: The Interpretation of Legal Texts 16 (2012) (emphasis added). If every single living American had been surveyed in 1964, it would have been hard to find any who thought that discrimination because of sex meant discrimination because of sexual orientation—not to mention gender identity, a concept that was essentially unknown at the time.

The Court attempts to pass off its decision as the inevitable product of the textualist school of statutory interpretation championed by our late colleague Justice Scalia, but no one should be fooled. The Court's opinion is like a pirate ship. It sails under a textualist flag, but what it actually represents is a theory of statutory interpretation that Justice Scalia excoriated—the theory that courts should "update" old statutes so that they better reflect the current values of society. See A. Scalia, A Matter of Interpretation 22 (1997). If the Court finds it appropriate to adopt this theory, it should own up to what it is doing.

Many will applaud today's decision because they agree on policy grounds with the Court's updating of Title VII. But the question in these cases is not whether discrimination because of sexual orientation or gender identity *should be* outlawed. The question is *whether Congress did that in 1964.*

---

[4]   Section 7(b) of H.R. 5 strikes the term "sex" in 42 U.S.C. § 2000e–2 and inserts: "SEX (INCLUDING SEXUAL ORIENTATION AND GENDER IDENTITY)."

It indisputably did not.

I

A

Title VII, as noted, prohibits discrimination "because of . . . sex," § 2000e–2(a)(1), and in 1964, it was as clear as clear could be that this meant discrimination because of the genetic and anatomical characteristics that men and women have at the time of birth. Determined searching has not found a single dictionary from that time that defined "sex" to mean sexual orientation, gender identity, or "transgender status."[6]

. . .

The Court does not dispute that this is what "sex" means in Title VII[.] . . .

If that is so, it should be perfectly clear that Title VII does not reach discrimination because of sexual orientation or gender identity. If "sex" in Title VII means biologically male or female, then discrimination because of sex means discrimination because the person in question is biologically male or biologically female, not because that person is sexually attracted to members of the same sex or identifies as a member of a particular gender.

. . .

Contrary to the Court's contention, discrimination because of sexual orientation or gender identity does not in and of itself entail discrimination because of sex. We can see this because it is quite possible for an employer to discriminate on those grounds without taking the sex of an individual applicant or employee into account. An employer can have a policy that says: "We do not hire gays, lesbians, or transgender individuals." And an employer can implement this policy without paying any attention to or even knowing the biological sex of gay, lesbian, and transgender applicants. . . .

At oral argument, the attorney representing the employees, a prominent professor of constitutional law, was asked if there would be discrimination because of sex if an employer with a blanket policy against hiring gays, lesbians, and transgender individuals implemented that policy without knowing the biological sex of any job applicants. Her

---

[6] The Court does not define what it means by "transgender status," but the American Psychological Association describes "transgender" as "[a]n umbrella term encompassing those whose gender identities or gender roles differ from those typically associated with the sex they were assigned at birth." A Glossary: Defining Transgender Terms, 49 Monitor on Psychology 32 (Sept. 2018), https://www.apa.org/monitor/2018/09/ce-corner-glossary. It defines "gender identity" as "[a]n internal sense of being male, female or something else, which may or may not correspond to an individual's sex assigned at birth or sex characteristics." Ibid. Under these definitions, there is no apparent difference between discrimination because of transgender status and discrimination because of gender identity.

candid answer was that this would "not" be sex discrimination.[10] And she was right.

The attorney's concession was necessary, but it is fatal to the Court's interpretation, for if an employer discriminates against individual applicants or employees without even knowing whether they are male or female, it is impossible to argue that the employer intentionally discriminated because of sex. An employer cannot intentionally discriminate on the basis of a characteristic of which the employer has no knowledge. And if an employer does not violate Title VII by discriminating on the basis of sexual orientation or gender identity without knowing the sex of the affected individuals, there is no reason why the same employer could not lawfully implement the same policy even if it knows the sex of these individuals. If an employer takes an adverse employment action for a perfectly legitimate reason—for example, because an employee stole company property—that action is not converted into sex discrimination simply because the employer knows the employee's sex. As explained, a disparate treatment case requires proof of intent—*i.e.*, that the employee's sex motivated the firing. In short, what this example shows is that discrimination because of sexual orientation or gender identity does not inherently or necessarily entail discrimination because of sex, and for that reason, the Court's chief argument collapses.

. . .

IV

What the Court has done today—interpreting discrimination because of "sex" to encompass discrimination because of sexual orientation or gender identity—is virtually certain to have far-reaching consequences. Over 100 federal statutes prohibit discrimination because of sex. . . . As to Title VII itself, the Court dismisses questions about "bathrooms, locker rooms, or anything else of the kind." And it declines to say anything about other statutes whose terms mirror Title VII's.

The Court's brusque refusal to consider the consequences of its reasoning is irresponsible. If the Court had allowed the legislative process to take its course, Congress would have had the opportunity to consider competing interests and might have found a way of accommodating at least some of them. In addition, Congress might have crafted special rules for some of the relevant statutes. But by intervening and proclaiming categorically that employment discrimination based on sexual orientation or gender identity is simply a form of discrimination because of sex, the Court has greatly impeded—and perhaps effectively ended—any chance of a bargained legislative resolution. Before issuing

---

[10] See Tr. of Oral Arg. in Nos. 17–1618, 17–1623, pp. 69–70 ("If there was that case, it might be the rare case in which sexual orientation discrimination is not a subset of sex"); see also *id.*, at 69 ("Somebody who comes in and says I'm not going to tell you what my sex is, but, believe me, I was fired for my sexual orientation, that person will lose").

today's radical decision, the Court should have given some thought to where its decision would lead.

As the briefing in these cases has warned, the position that the Court now adopts will threaten freedom of religion, freedom of speech, and personal privacy and safety. No one should think that the Court's decision represents an unalloyed victory for individual liberty.

I will briefly note some of the potential consequences of the Court's decision, but I do not claim to provide a comprehensive survey or to suggest how any of these issues should necessarily play out under the Court's reasoning.[43]

"[B]athrooms, locker rooms, [and other things] of [that] kind." The Court may wish to avoid this subject, but it is a matter of concern to many people who are reticent about disrobing or using toilet facilities in the presence of individuals whom they regard as members of the opposite sex. For some, this may simply be a question of modesty, but for others, there is more at stake. For women who have been victimized by sexual assault or abuse, the experience of seeing an unclothed person with the anatomy of a male in a confined and sensitive location such as a bathroom or locker room can cause serious psychological harm.[44]

Under the Court's decision, however, transgender persons will be able to argue that they are entitled to use a bathroom or locker room that is reserved for persons of the sex with which they identify, and while the Court does not define what it means by a transgender person, the term may apply to individuals who are "gender fluid," that is, individuals whose gender identity is mixed or changes over time.[45] Thus, a person who has not undertaken any physical transitioning may claim the right to use the bathroom or locker room assigned to the sex with which the individual identifies at that particular time. The Court provides no clue why a transgender person's claim to such bathroom or locker room access might not succeed.

A similar issue has arisen under Title IX, which prohibits sex discrimination by any elementary or secondary school and any college or university that receives federal financial assistance.[46] In 2016, a Department of Justice advisory warned that barring a student from a bathroom assigned to individuals of the gender with which the student

---

[43] Contrary to the implication in the Court's opinion, I do not label these potential consequences "undesirable." I mention them only as possible implications of the Court's reasoning.

[44] Brief for Defend My Privacy et al. as *Amici Curiae* 7–10.

[45] See 1 Sadock, Comprehensive Textbook of Psychiatry, at 2063 (explaining that "gender is now often regarded as more *fluid*" and "[t]hus, gender identity may be described as masculine, feminine, or somewhere in between").

[46] Title IX makes it unlawful to discriminate on the basis of sex in education: "No person in the United States shall, on the basis of sex, be excluded from participation in, be denied the benefits of, or be subjected to discrimination under any education program or activity receiving Federal financial assistance." 20 U.S.C. § 1681(a).

identifies constitutes unlawful sex discrimination,[47] and some lower court decisions have agreed. See *Whitaker v. Kenosha Unified School Dist. No. 1 Bd. of Ed.*, 858 F.3d 1034, 1049 (CA7 2017); *G. G. v. Gloucester Cty. School Bd.*, 822 F.3d 709, 715 (CA4 2016), vacated and remanded, 580 U.S. ___, 137 S.Ct. 1239 (2017); *Adams v. School Bd. of St. Johns Cty.*, 318 F.Supp.3d 1293, 1325 (MD Fla. 2018); cf. *Doe v. Boyertown Area School Dist.*, 897 F.3d 518, 533 (CA3 2018), cert. denied, 587 U.S. ___, 139 S.Ct. 2636 (2019).

. . .

Constitutional claims. Finally, despite the important differences between the Fourteenth Amendment and Title VII, the Court's decision may exert a gravitational pull in constitutional cases. Under our precedents, the Equal Protection Clause prohibits sex-based discrimination unless a "heightened" standard of review is met. *Sessions v. Morales-Santana*, 582 U.S. ___, ___, 137 S.Ct. 1678, 1689 (2017); *United States v. Virginia*, 518 U.S. 515, 532–534 (1996). By equating discrimination because of sexual orientation or gender identity with discrimination because of sex, the Court's decision will be cited as a ground for subjecting all three forms of discrimination to the same exacting standard of review.

Under this logic, today's decision may have effects that extend well beyond the domain of federal antidiscrimination statutes. This potential is illustrated by pending and recent lower court cases in which transgender individuals have challenged a variety of federal, state, and local laws and policies on constitutional grounds. See, *e.g.*, Complaint in *Hecox* [*v. Little*], No. 1: 20–CV–00184 [(D. Idaho, Apr. 15, 2020)] (state law prohibiting transgender students from competing in school sports in accordance with their gender identity); Second Amended Complaint in *Karnoski v. Trump*, No. 2:17–cv–01297 (WD Wash., July 31, 2019) (military's ban on transgender members); *Kadel v. Folwell*, [446 F.Supp.3d 1, 10–11] (M[.]D[.]N[.]C[.], 2020) (state health plan's exclusion of coverage for sex reassignment procedures); Complaint in *Gore v. Lee*, No. 3:19–cv–00328 (MD Tenn., Mar. 3, 2020) (change of gender on birth certificates); Brief for Appellee in *Grimm v. Gloucester Cty. School Bd.*, No. 19–1952 (CA4, Nov. 18, 2019) (transgender student forced to use gender neutral bathrooms at school); Complaint in *Corbitt v. Taylor*, No. 2:18–cv–00091 (MD Ala., July 25, 2018) (change of gender on driver's licenses); *Whitaker*, 858 F.3d at 1054 (school policy requiring students to use the bathroom that corresponds to the sex on birth certificate); *Keohane v. Florida Dept. of Corrections Secretary*, 952 F.3d 1257, 1262–1265 (CA11 2020) (transgender prisoner denied hormone therapy and ability to dress and groom as a female); *Edmo v. Corizon, Inc.*, 935 F.3d 757, 767 (CA9 2019) (transgender prisoner requested sex reassignment

---

[47] See Dept. of Justice & Dept. of Education, Dear Colleague Letter on Transgender Students, May 13, 2016 (Dear Colleague Letter), https://www2.ed.gov/about/offices/list/ocr/letters/colleague-201605-title-ix-transgender.pdf.

surgery); cf. *Glenn v. Brumby*, 663 F.3d 1312, 1320 (CA11 2011) (transgender individual fired for gender non-conformity).

Although the Court does not want to think about the consequences of its decision, we will not be able to avoid those issues for long. The entire Federal Judiciary will be mired for years in disputes about the reach of the Court's reasoning.

* * *

The updating desire to which the Court succumbs no doubt arises from humane and generous impulses. Today, many Americans know individuals who are gay, lesbian, or transgender and want them to be treated with the dignity, consideration, and fairness that everyone deserves. But the authority of this Court is limited to saying what the law *is*.

The Court itself recognizes this:

"The place to make new legislation . . . lies in Congress. When it comes to statutory interpretation, our role is limited to applying the law's demands as faithfully as we can in the cases that come before us." *Ante*, at ___.

It is easy to utter such words. If only the Court would live by them.

I respectfully dissent.

■ JUSTICE KAVANAUGH, dissenting.

Like many cases in this Court, this case boils down to one fundamental question: Who decides? Title VII of the Civil Rights Act of 1964 prohibits employment discrimination "because of" an individual's "race, color, religion, sex, or national origin." The question here is whether Title VII should be expanded to prohibit employment discrimination because of sexual orientation. Under the Constitution's separation of powers, the responsibility to amend Title VII belongs to Congress and the President in the legislative process, not to this Court.

The political branches are well aware of this issue. . . .

The policy arguments for amending Title VII are very weighty. . . .

But we are judges, not Members of Congress. . . . Our role is not to make or amend the law. As written, Title VII does not prohibit employment discrimination because of sexual orientation.[1]

. . .

II

. . .

. . . [T]his case involves sexual orientation discrimination, which has long and widely been understood as distinct from, and not a form of, sex

---

[1] Although this opinion does not separately analyze discrimination on the basis of gender identity, this opinion's legal analysis of discrimination on the basis of sexual orientation would apply in much the same way to discrimination on the basis of gender identity.

discrimination. Until now, federal law has always reflected that common usage and recognized that distinction between sex discrimination and sexual orientation discrimination. To fire one employee because she is a woman and another employee because he is gay implicates two distinct societal concerns, reveals two distinct biases, imposes two distinct harms, and falls within two distinct statutory prohibitions.

. . .

As a result, many Americans will not buy the novel interpretation unearthed and advanced by the Court today. . . .

I have the greatest, and unyielding, respect for my colleagues and for their good faith. But when this Court usurps the role of Congress, as it does today, the public understandably becomes confused about who the policymakers really are in our system of separated powers, and inevitably becomes cynical about the oft-repeated aspiration that judges base their decisions on law rather than on personal preference. The best way for judges to demonstrate that we are deciding cases based on the ordinary meaning of the law is to walk the walk, even in the hard cases when we might prefer a different policy outcome.

* * *

. . .

Notwithstanding my concern about the Court's transgression of the Constitution's separation of powers, it is appropriate to acknowledge the important victory achieved today by gay and lesbian Americans. Millions of gay and lesbian Americans have worked hard for many decades to achieve equal treatment in fact and in law. They have exhibited extraordinary vision, tenacity, and grit—battling often steep odds in the legislative and judicial arenas, not to mention in their daily lives. They have advanced powerful policy arguments and can take pride in today's result. Under the Constitution's separation of powers, however, I believe that it was Congress's role, not this Court's, to amend Title VII. I therefore must respectfully dissent from the Court's judgment.

Note

How does *Bostock* and the controversy it involves relate to family law and family welfare? Is *Bostock* practically conceivable without the Supreme Court's LGBT rights decisions leading up to and culminating in *Obergefell v. Hodges*? For discussion, see generally Marc Spindelman, Bostock's *Paradox: Textualism, Legal Justice, and the Constitution*, 69 Buff. L. Rev. 553 (2021). Is *Bostock* imaginable as a sex discrimination ruling in the absence of the Supreme Court's earlier constitutional and statutory sex discrimination cases? For some relevant discussion of the case along these lines, see Ann C. McGinley et al., *Feminist Perspectives on* Bostock v. Clayton County, 53 Conn. L. Rev. Online 1, 12 (2020). How do the opinions in *Bostock* differentially make work and life opportunities available to different workers, households, and families? Looking to other family law developments in its aftermath, how does *Bostock* relate to the Supreme Court's recent decision in *Dobbs v. Jackson Women's Health Org.* below? Can the two rulings easily be squared, or are there tensions, perhaps even deep tensions, between them?

C. THE DOCTRINE OF FAMILY PRIVACY, AGAIN

1. THE CONSTITUTIONAL "RIGHT TO PRIVACY" (A.K.A. CONSTITUTIONALLY-PROTECTED "LIBERTY")

On page 277 of the Unabridged 7th edition, and on page 217 of the Concise 7th edition, immediately after *Planned Parenthood v. Casey*, substitute the following text, while also deleting *Whole Woman's Health v. Hellerstedt*:

Dobbs v. Jackson Women's Health Org.

Supreme Court of the United States, 2022.
597 U.S. ___, 142 S.Ct. 2228, ___ L.Ed. ___.

■ JUSTICE ALITO delivered the opinion of the Court.

. . .

. . . The State of Mississippi asks us to uphold the constitutionality of a law that generally prohibits an abortion after the 15th week of pregnancy[.] . . . [T]he State's primary argument is that we should reconsider and overrule *Roe* [*v. Wade*, 410 U.S. 113 (1973)] and [*Planned Parenthood of Southeastern Pa. v.*] *Casey*[, 505 U.S. 833 (1992)] and once again allow each State to regulate abortion as its citizens wish. . . .

We hold that *Roe* and *Casey* must be overruled.

. . .

It is time to heed the Constitution and return the issue of abortion to the people's elected representatives. . . . That is what the Constitution and the rule of law demand.

. . .

II

We begin by considering the critical question whether the Constitution, properly understood, confers a right to obtain an abortion. . . .

A

1

Constitutional analysis must begin with "the language of the instrument[.]" *Gibbons v. Ogden*, 9 Wheat. 1, 186–189 (1824)[.] . . . The Constitution makes no express reference to a right to obtain an abortion, and therefore those who claim that it protects such a right must show that the right is somehow implicit in the constitutional text.

Roe, however, was remarkably loose in its treatment of the constitutional text. It held that the abortion right, which is not mentioned in the Constitution, is part of a right to privacy, which is also not mentioned. . . .

. . . The *Casey* Court did not defend this unfocused analysis and instead grounded its decision solely on the theory that the right to obtain an abortion is part of the "liberty" protected by the Fourteenth Amendment's Due Process Clause.

. . . [B]efore [discussing this theory] . . ., we briefly address . . . the Fourteenth Amendment's Equal Protection Clause. Neither *Roe* nor *Casey* saw fit to invoke this theory [that the abortion right is founded in the Equal Protection Clause as a basis for its conclusion], and it is squarely foreclosed by our precedents, which establish that a State's regulation of abortion is not a sex-based classification and is thus not subject to the "heightened scrutiny" that applies to such classifications. The regulation of a medical procedure that only one sex can undergo does not trigger heightened constitutional scrutiny unless the regulation is a "mere pretex[t] designed to effect an invidious discrimination against members of one sex or the other." *Geduldig v. Aiello*, 417 U.S. 484, 496, n. 20 (1974). And as the Court has stated, the "goal of preventing abortion" does not constitute "invidiously discriminatory animus" against women. *Bray v. Alexandria Women's Health Clinic*, 506 U.S. 263, 273–274 (1993) (internal quotation marks omitted). Accordingly, laws regulating or prohibiting abortion are not subject to heightened scrutiny. Rather, they are governed by the same standard of review as other health and safety measures.

. . . [W]e [now] turn to *Casey*'s bold assertion that the abortion right is an aspect of the "liberty" protected by the Due Process Clause of the Fourteenth Amendment.

2

The underlying theory on which this argument rests—that the Fourteenth Amendment's Due Process Clause provides substantive, as well as procedural, protection for "liberty"—has long been controversial. But our decisions have held that the Due Process Clause protects . . . a select list of fundamental rights that are not mentioned anywhere in the Constitution.

. . . [T]he Court has long asked whether the right is "deeply rooted in [our] history and tradition" and whether it is essential to our Nation's "scheme of ordered liberty." *Timbs v. Indiana*, 586 U.S. ___, ___, 139 S.Ct. 682, 686 (2019) (internal quotation marks omitted); *McDonald [v. Chicago]*, 561 U.S. [742,] 764, 767 [(2010)] (internal quotation marks omitted); [*Washington v.*] *Glucksberg*, 521 U.S. [702,] 721 [(1997)] (internal quotation marks omitted). And in conducting this inquiry, we have engaged in a careful analysis of the history of the right at issue.

. . .

B

1

Until the latter part of the 20th century, there was no support in American law for a constitutional right to obtain an abortion. No state constitutional provision had recognized such a right. Until a few years before *Roe* was handed down, no federal or state court had recognized such a right. Nor had any scholarly treatise of which we are aware. And although law review articles are not reticent about advocating new rights, the earliest article proposing a constitutional right to abortion that has come to our attention was published only a few years before *Roe*.

Not only was there no support for such a constitutional right until shortly before *Roe*, but abortion had long been a *crime* in every single State. At common law, abortion was criminal in at least some stages of pregnancy and was regarded as unlawful and could have very serious consequences at all stages. American law followed the common law until a wave of statutory restrictions in the 1800s expanded criminal liability for abortions. By the time of the adoption of the Fourteenth Amendment, three-quarters of the States had made abortion a crime at any stage of pregnancy, and the remaining States would soon follow.

Roe either ignored or misstated this history, and *Casey* declined to reconsider *Roe*'s faulty historical analysis. . . .

2

a

We begin with the common law, under which abortion was a crime at least after "quickening"—*i.e.*, the first felt movement of the fetus in the womb, which usually occurs between the 16th and 18th week of pregnancy.

The "eminent common-law authorities (Blackstone, Coke, Hale, and the like)," *Kahler v. Kansas*, 589 U.S. ___, ___, 140 S.Ct. 1021, 1027 (2020), *all* describe abortion after quickening as criminal. . . .

. . .

English cases dating all the way back to the 13th century corroborate the treatises' statements that abortion was a crime. . . .

Although a pre-quickening abortion was not itself considered homicide, it does not follow that abortion was *permissible* at common law—much less that abortion was a legal *right*. . . .

. . .

. . . [A]lthough common-law authorities differed on the severity of punishment for abortions committed at different points in pregnancy, none endorsed the practice. Moreover, we are aware of no common-law case or authority, and the parties have not pointed to any, that remotely suggests a positive *right* to procure an abortion at any stage of pregnancy.

b

In this country, the historical record is similar. The "most important early American edition of Blackstone's Commentaries," *District of Columbia v. Heller*, 554 U.S. 570, 594 (2008), reported Blackstone's statement that abortion of a quick child was at least "a heinous misdemeanor," 2 St. George Tucker, Blackstone's Commentaries 129–130 (1803)[.] . . . Manuals for justices of the peace printed in the Colonies in the 18th century typically restated the common-law rule on abortion, and some manuals repeated Hale's and Blackstone's statements that anyone who prescribed medication "unlawfully to destroy the child" would be guilty of murder if the woman died. See, *e.g.*, J. Parker, Conductor Generalis 220 (1788); 2 R. Burn, Justice of the Peace, and Parish Officer 221–222 (7th ed. 1762) (English manual stating the same).

The few cases available from the early colonial period corroborate that abortion was a crime. See generally Dellapenna 215–228 (collecting cases). In Maryland in 1652, for example, an indictment charged that a man "Murtherously endeavoured to destroy or Murther the Child by him begotten in the Womb." *Proprietary v. Mitchell*, 10 Md. Archives 80, 183 (1652) (W. Browne ed. 1891). And by the 19th century, courts frequently explained that the common law made abortion of a quick child a crime. See, *e.g.*, *Smith v. Gaffard*, 31 Ala. 45, 51 (1857); *Smith v. State*, 33 Me. 48, 55 (1851); *State v. Cooper*, 22 N.J.L. 52, 52–55 (1849); *Commonwealth v. Parker*, 50 Mass. 263, 264–268 (1845).

c

The original ground for drawing a distinction between pre- and post-quickening abortions is not entirely clear[.] . . .

. . .

At any rate, the original ground for the quickening rule is of little importance for present purposes because the rule was abandoned in the 19th century. . . .

In this country during the 19th century, the vast majority of the States enacted statutes criminalizing abortion at all stages of pregnancy. By 1868, the year when the Fourteenth Amendment was ratified, three-quarters of the States, 28 out of 37, had enacted statutes making abortion a crime even if it was performed before quickening. Of the nine States that had not yet criminalized abortion at all stages, all but one did so by 1910.

The trend in the Territories that would become the last 13 States was similar: All of them criminalized abortion at all stages of pregnancy between 1850 (the Kingdom of Hawaii) and 1919 (New Mexico). By the end of the 1950s, according to the *Roe* Court's own count, statutes in all but four States and the District of Columbia prohibited abortion "however and whenever performed, unless done to save or preserve the life of the mother." 410 U.S. at 139.

This overwhelming consensus endured until the day *Roe* was decided. At that time, also by the *Roe* Court's own count, a substantial majority—30 States—still prohibited abortion at all stages except to save the life of the mother. See *id.*, at 118, and n. 2 (listing States). And though *Roe* discerned a "trend toward liberalization" in about "one-third of the States," those States still criminalized some abortions and regulated them more stringently than *Roe* would allow. *Id.*, at 140, and n. 37. In short, the "Court's opinion in *Roe* itself convincingly refutes the notion that the abortion liberty is deeply rooted in the history or tradition of our people." *Thornburgh v. American College of Obstetricians and Gynecologists*, 476 U.S. 747, 793 (1986) (White, J., dissenting).

d

The inescapable conclusion is that a right to abortion is not deeply rooted in the Nation's history and traditions. On the contrary, an unbroken tradition of prohibiting abortion on pain of criminal punishment persisted from the earliest days of the common law until 1973. . . .

3

Respondents and their *amici* have no persuasive answer to this historical evidence.

Neither respondents nor the Solicitor General disputes the fact that by 1868 the vast majority of States criminalized abortion at all stages of pregnancy. Instead, respondents are forced to argue that it "does [not] matter that some States prohibited abortion at the time *Roe* was decided or when the Fourteenth Amendment was adopted." Brief for Respondents 21. But that argument flies in the face of the standard we have applied in determining whether an asserted right that is nowhere mentioned in the Constitution is nevertheless protected by the Fourteenth Amendment.

Not only are respondents and their *amici* unable to show that a constitutional right to abortion was established when the Fourteenth Amendment was adopted, but they have found no support for the existence of an abortion right that predates the latter part of the 20th century—no state constitutional provision, no statute, no judicial decision, no learned treatise. The earliest sources called to our attention are a few district court and state court decisions decided shortly before *Roe* and a small number of law review articles from the same time period. . . .

C

1

Instead of seriously pressing the argument that the abortion right itself has deep roots, supporters of *Roe* and *Casey* contend that the abortion right is an integral part of a broader entrenched right. *Roe* termed this a right to privacy, 410 U.S. at 154, and *Casey* described it as the freedom to make "intimate and personal choices" that are "central to personal dignity and autonomy," 505 U.S. at 851. *Casey* elaborated: "At the heart of liberty is the right to define one's own concept of existence, of meaning, of the universe, and of the mystery of human life." *Ibid.*

The Court did not claim that this broadly framed right is absolute, and no such claim would be plausible. While individuals are certainly free *to think* and *to say* what they wish about "existence," "meaning," the "universe," and "the mystery of human life," they are not always free *to act* in accordance with those thoughts. License to act on the basis of such beliefs may correspond to one of the many understandings of "liberty," but it is certainly not "ordered liberty."

Ordered liberty sets limits and defines the boundary between competing interests. *Roe* and *Casey* each struck a particular balance between the interests of a woman who wants an abortion and the interests of what they termed "potential life." *Roe*, 410 U.S. at 150 (emphasis deleted); *Casey*, 505 U.S. at 852. But the people of the various States may evaluate those interests differently. In some States, voters may believe that the abortion right should be even more extensive than the right that *Roe* and *Casey* recognized. Voters in other States may wish to impose tight restrictions based on their belief that abortion destroys an "unborn human being." Miss. Code Ann. § 41–41–191(4)(b). Our Nation's historical understanding of ordered liberty does not prevent the people's elected representatives from deciding how abortion should be regulated.

Nor does the right to obtain an abortion have a sound basis in precedent. *Casey* relied on cases involving the right to marry a person of a different race, *Loving v. Virginia*, 388 U.S. 1 (1967); the right to marry while in prison, *Turner v. Safley*, 482 U.S. 78 (1987); the right to obtain contraceptives, *Griswold v. Connecticut*, 381 U.S. 479 (1965), *Eisenstadt v. Baird*, 405 U.S. 438 (1972), *Carey v. Population Services Int'l*, 431 U.S. 678 (1977); the right to reside with relatives, *Moore v. East Cleveland*, 431 U.S. 494 (1977); the right to make decisions about the education of one's children, *Pierce v. Society of Sisters* (1925), *Meyer v. Nebraska*, 262 U.S. 390 (1923); the right not to be sterilized without consent, *Skinner v. Oklahoma ex rel. Williamson*, 316 U.S. 535 (1942); and the right in certain circumstances not to undergo involuntary surgery, forced administration of drugs, or other substantially similar procedures, *Winston v. Lee*, 470 U.S. 753 (1985), *Washington v. Harper*, 494 U.S. 210 (1990), *Rochin v. California*, 342 U.S. 165 (1952). Respondents and the Solicitor General also rely on post-*Casey* decisions like *Lawrence v. Texas*, 539 U.S. 558 (2003) (right to engage in private, consensual sexual acts), and *Obergefell v. Hodges*, 576 U.S. 644 (2015) (right to marry a person of the same sex).

These attempts to justify abortion through appeals to a broader right to autonomy and to define one's "concept of existence" prove too much. *Casey*, 505 U.S. at 851. Those criteria, at a high level of generality, could license fundamental rights to illicit drug use, prostitution, and the like. None of these rights has any claim to being deeply rooted in history.

What sharply distinguishes the abortion right from the rights recognized in the cases on which *Roe* and *Casey* rely is something that both those decisions acknowledged: Abortion destroys what those decisions call "potential life" and what the law at issue in this case regards as the life of an "unborn human being." See *Roe*, 410 U.S. at 159 (abortion is "inherently different"); *Casey*, 505 U.S. at 852 (abortion is "a unique act"). None of the other decisions cited by *Roe* and *Casey* involved the critical moral question posed by abortion. They are therefore inapposite. They do not support the right to obtain an abortion, and by the same token, our conclusion that the Constitution does not confer such a right does not undermine them in any way.

. . .

D

III

We next consider whether the doctrine of *stare decisis* counsels continued acceptance of *Roe* and *Casey*. *Stare decisis* plays an important role in our case law[.] . . . It protects the interests of those who have taken action in reliance on a past decision. . . . It "contributes to the actual and perceived integrity of the judicial process." [*Payne v. Tennessee*, 501 U.S. 808, 827 (1991).] And it restrains judicial hubris and reminds us to respect the judgment of those who have grappled with important questions in the past. . . .

We have long recognized, however, that *stare decisis* is "not an inexorable command[.]" *Pearson v. Callahan*, 555 U.S. 223, 233 (2009) (internal quotation marks omitted). . . .

. . .

In this case, five factors weigh strongly in favor of overruling *Roe* and *Casey*: the nature of their error, the quality of their reasoning, the "workability" of the rules they imposed on the country, their disruptive effect on other areas of the law, and the absence of concrete reliance.

A

The nature of the Court's error. . . .

. . .

Roe was also egregiously wrong and deeply damaging. . . . *Roe*'s constitutional analysis was far outside the bounds of any reasonable interpretation of the various constitutional provisions to which it vaguely pointed.

Roe was on a collision course with the Constitution from the day it was decided, *Casey* perpetuated its errors[.] . . . [W]ielding nothing but "raw judicial power," *Roe*, 410 U.S. at 222 (White, J., dissenting), the Court usurped the power to address a question of profound moral and social importance that the Constitution unequivocally leaves for the people. . . .

. . .

B

The quality of the reasoning. Under our precedents, the quality of the reasoning in a prior case has an important bearing on whether it should be reconsidered. . . .

Roe found that the Constitution implicitly conferred a right to obtain an abortion, but it failed to ground its decision in text, history, or precedent. It relied on an erroneous historical narrative; it devoted great attention to and presumably relied on matters that have no bearing on the meaning of the Constitution; it disregarded the fundamental difference between the precedents on which it relied and the question before the Court; it concocted an elaborate set of rules, with different restrictions for each trimester of pregnancy, but it did not explain how this veritable code could be teased out of anything in the Constitution, the history of abortion laws, prior precedent, or any other cited source; and its most important rule (that States cannot protect fetal life prior to "viability") was never raised by any party and has never been plausibly explained. *Roe*'s reasoning quickly drew scathing scholarly criticism, even from supporters of broad access to abortion.

The *Casey* plurality, while reaffirming *Roe*'s central holding, pointedly refrained from endorsing most of its reasoning. It revised the textual basis for the abortion right, silently abandoned *Roe*'s erroneous historical narrative, and jettisoned the trimester framework. But it replaced that scheme with an arbitrary "undue burden" test and relied on an exceptional version of *stare decisis* that, as explained below, this Court had never before applied and has never invoked since.

. . .

2

When *Casey* revisited *Roe* almost 20 years later, very little of *Roe*'s reasoning was defended or preserved. The Court abandoned any reliance on a privacy right and instead grounded the abortion right entirely on the Fourteenth Amendment's Due Process Clause. The Court did not reaffirm *Roe*'s erroneous account of abortion history. In fact, none of the Justices in the majority said anything about the history of the abortion right. And as for precedent, the Court relied on essentially the same body of cases that *Roe* had cited. Thus, with respect to the standard grounds for constitutional decisionmaking—text, history, and precedent—*Casey* did not attempt to bolster *Roe*'s reasoning.

The Court also made no real effort to remedy one of the greatest weaknesses in *Roe*'s analysis: its much-criticized discussion of viability. The Court retained what it called *Roe*'s "central holding"—that a State may not regulate pre-viability abortions for the purpose of protecting fetal life—but it provided no principled defense of the viability line. 505 U.S. at 860, 870–871. Instead, it merely rephrased what *Roe* had said, stating that viability marked the point at which "the independent existence of a second life can in reason and fairness be the object of state protection that now overrides the rights of the woman." [*Id.,*] at 870. Why "reason and fairness" demanded that the line be drawn at viability the Court did not explain. And the Justices who authored the controlling opinion conspicuously failed to say that they agreed with the viability rule; instead, they candidly acknowledged "the reservations [some] of us may have in reaffirming [that] holding of *Roe.*" *Id.,* at 853.

The controlling opinion criticized and rejected *Roe's* trimester scheme, [*id.,*] at 872, and substituted a new "undue burden" test, but the basis for this test was obscure. . . .

Casey, in short, either refused to reaffirm or rejected important aspects of *Roe's* analysis, failed to remedy glaring deficiencies in *Roe's* reasoning, endorsed what it termed *Roe's* central holding while suggesting that a majority might not have thought it was correct, provided no new support for the abortion right other than *Roe's* status as precedent, and imposed a new and problematic test with no firm grounding in constitutional text, history, or precedent.

As discussed below, *Casey* also deployed a novel version of the doctrine of *stare decisis*. This new doctrine did not account for the profound wrongness of the decision in *Roe*, and placed great weight on an intangible form of reliance with little if any basis in prior case law. *Stare decisis* does not command the preservation of such a decision.

C

Workability. Our precedents counsel that another important consideration in deciding whether a precedent should be overruled is whether the rule it imposes is workable—that is, whether it can be understood and applied in a consistent and predictable manner. *Casey's* "undue burden" test has scored poorly on the workability scale.

1

Problems begin with the very concept of an "undue burden." . . . [D]etermining whether a burden is "due" or "undue" is "inherently standardless." 505 U.S. at 992.

. . .

2

. . .

The ambiguity of the "undue burden" test also produced disagreement in later cases. In *Whole Woman's Health* [*v. Hellerstedt*], the Court adopted the cost-benefit interpretation of the test, stating that "[t]he rule announced in *Casey* . . . requires that courts consider the burdens a law imposes on abortion access *together with the benefits those laws confer.*" [579 U.S. 582, 607 (2016)] (emphasis added). But five years later, a majority of the Justices rejected that interpretation. See *June Medical* [*Services v. Russo*], 591 U.S. ___, 140 S.Ct. 2103 [(2020)]. Four Justices reaffirmed *Whole Woman's Health*'s instruction to "weigh" a law's "benefits" against "the burdens it imposes on abortion access." 591 U.S., at ___, 140 S.Ct., at 2135 (plurality opinion) (internal quotation marks omitted). But THE CHIEF JUSTICE—who cast the deciding vote—argued that "[n]othing about *Casey* suggested that a weighing of costs and benefits of an abortion regulation was a job for the courts." *Id.,* at ___, 140 S.Ct., at 2136 (opinion concurring in judgment). And the four Justices in dissent rejected the plurality's interpretation of *Casey*. See 591 U.S., at ___, 140 S.Ct., at 2154–2155 (opinion of ALITO, J., joined in relevant part by THOMAS, GORSUCH, and KAVANAUGH, JJ.); *id.,* at ___–___, 140 S.Ct., at 2178–2180 (opinion of GORSUCH, J.); *id.,* at ___–___, 140 S.Ct., at 2182 (opinion of KAVANAUGH, J.) ("[F]ive Members of the Court reject the *Whole Woman's Health* cost-benefit standard").

This Court's experience applying *Casey* has confirmed Chief Justice Rehnquist's prescient diagnosis that the undue-burden standard was "not built to last." *Casey*, 505 U.S. at 965 (opinion concurring in judgment in part and dissenting in part).

3

The experience of the Courts of Appeals provides further evidence that *Casey*'s "line between" permissible and unconstitutional restrictions "has proved to be impossible to draw with precision." *Janus* [*v. State, County, and Municipal Employees*], 585 U.S. ___, ___, 138 S.Ct. [2448], 2481 [(2018)].

Casey has generated a long list of Circuit conflicts. . . .

. . .

Casey's "undue burden" test has proved to be unworkable. "[P]lucked from nowhere," [*Casey*,] 505 U.S. at 965 (opinion of Rehnquist, C. J.), it "seems calculated to perpetuate give-it-a-try litigation" before judges assigned an unwieldy and inappropriate task. *Lehnert v. Ferris Faculty Assn.*, 500 U.S. 507, 551 (1991) (Scalia, J., concurring in judgment in part and dissenting in part). Continued adherence to that standard would undermine, not advance, the "evenhanded, predictable, and consistent development of legal principles." *Payne*, 501 U.S. at 827.

D

Effect on other areas of law. Roe and *Casey* have led to the distortion of many important but unrelated legal doctrines, and that effect provides further support for overruling those decisions. See *Ramos* [*v. Louisiana*], 590 U.S. ___, ___, 140 S.Ct., at 1397–98 [(2020)] (opinion of KAVANAUGH, J.); *Janus*, 585 U.S., at ___, 138 S.Ct., at 2478.

Members of this Court have repeatedly lamented that "no legal rule or doctrine is safe from ad hoc nullification by this Court when an occasion for its application arises in a case involving state regulation of abortion." *Thornburgh*, 476 U.S. at 814 (O'Connor, J., dissenting); see *Madsen v. Women's Health Center, Inc.*, 512 U.S. 753, 785 (1994) (Scalia, J., concurring in judgment in part and dissenting in part); *Whole Woman's Health*, 579 U.S. at 631–633 (THOMAS, J., dissenting); *id.*, at 645–666, 678–684 (ALITO, J., dissenting); *June Medical*, 591 U.S., at ___–___, 140 S.Ct., at 2171–2179 (GORSUCH, J., dissenting).

The Court's abortion cases have diluted the strict standard for facial constitutional challenges. They have ignored the Court's third-party standing doctrine. They have disregarded standard *res judicata* principles. They have flouted the ordinary rules on the severability of unconstitutional provisions, as well as the rule that statutes should be read where possible to avoid unconstitutionality. And they have distorted First Amendment doctrines.

When vindicating a doctrinal innovation requires courts to engineer exceptions to longstanding background rules, the doctrine "has failed to deliver the 'principled and intelligible' development of the law that *stare decisis* purports to secure." *Id.*, at ___, 140 S.Ct., at 2152 (THOMAS, J., dissenting) (quoting *Vasquez v. Hillery*, 474 U.S. 254, 265 (1986)).

E

Reliance interests. We last consider whether overruling *Roe* and *Casey* will upend substantial reliance interests.

1

Traditional reliance interests arise "where advance planning of great precision is most obviously a necessity." *Casey*, 505 U.S. at 856 (joint opinion). In *Casey*, the controlling opinion conceded that those traditional reliance interests were not implicated because getting an abortion is generally "unplanned activity," and "reproductive planning could take virtually immediate account of any sudden restoration of state authority to ban abortions." 505 U.S. at 856. For these reasons, we agree with the *Casey* plurality that conventional, concrete reliance interests are not present here.

. . .

2

. . .

Our decision returns the issue of abortion to . . . legislative bodies, and it allows women on both sides of the abortion issue to seek to affect the legislative process by influencing public opinion, lobbying legislators, voting, and running for office. Women are not without electoral or political power. It is noteworthy that the percentage of women who register to vote and cast ballots is consistently higher than the percentage of men who do so. In the last election in November 2020, women, who make up around 51.5 percent of the population of Mississippi, constituted 55.5 percent of the voters who cast ballots.

3

Unable to show concrete reliance on *Roe* and *Casey* themselves, the Solicitor General suggests that overruling those decisions would "threaten the Court's precedents holding that the Due Process Clause protects other rights." Brief for United States 26 (citing *Obergefell*, 576 U.S. 644; *Lawrence*, 539 U.S. 558; *Griswold*, 381 U.S. 479). That is not correct[.] . . . As even the *Casey* plurality recognized, "[a]bortion is a unique act" because it terminates "life or potential life." 505 U.S. at 852; see also *Roe*, 410 U.S. at 159 (abortion is "inherently different from marital intimacy," "marriage," or "procreation"). And to ensure that our decision is not misunderstood or mischaracterized, we emphasize that our decision concerns the constitutional right to abortion and no other right. Nothing in this opinion should be understood to cast doubt on precedents that do not concern abortion.

IV

Having shown that traditional *stare decisis* factors do not weigh in favor of retaining *Roe* or *Casey*, we must address one final argument that featured prominently in the *Casey* plurality opinion.

The argument was cast in different terms, but stated simply, it was essentially as follows. The American people's belief in the rule of law would be shaken if they lost respect for this Court as an institution that decides important cases based on principle, not "social and political pressures." 505 U.S. at 865. There is a special danger that the public will perceive a decision as having been made for unprincipled reasons when the Court overrules a controversial "watershed" decision, such as *Roe*. 505 U.S. at 866–867. A decision overruling *Roe* would be perceived as having been made "under fire" and as a "surrender to political pressure," 505 U.S. at 867, and therefore the preservation of public approval of the Court weighs heavily in favor of retaining *Roe*, see 505 U.S. at 869.

This analysis starts out on the right foot but ultimately veers off course. The *Casey* plurality was certainly right that it is important for the public to perceive that our decisions are based on principle, and we should make every effort to achieve that objective by issuing opinions that carefully show how a proper understanding of the law leads to the results we reach. But we cannot exceed the scope of our authority under the Constitution, and we cannot allow our decisions to be affected by any extraneous influences such as concern about the public's reaction to our work. That is true both when we initially decide a constitutional issue *and* when we consider whether to overrule a prior decision. . . . In suggesting otherwise, the *Casey* plurality went beyond this Court's role in our constitutional system.

. . .

The *Casey* plurality also misjudged the practical limits of this Court's influence. *Roe* certainly did not succeed in ending division on the issue of abortion. On the contrary, *Roe* "inflamed" a national issue that has remained bitterly divisive for the past half century. *Casey*, 505 U.S. at 995 (opinion of Scalia, J.). And for the past 30 years, *Casey* has done the same.

Neither decision has ended debate over the issue of a constitutional right to obtain an abortion. Indeed, in this case, 26 States expressly ask us to overrule *Roe* and *Casey* and to return the issue of abortion to the people and their elected representatives. This Court's inability to end debate on the issue should not have been surprising. This Court cannot bring about the permanent resolution of a rancorous national controversy simply by dictating a settlement and telling the people to move on. Whatever influence the Court may have on public attitudes must stem from the strength of our opinions, not an attempt to exercise "raw judicial power." *Roe*, 410 U.S. at 222 (White, J., dissenting).

We do not pretend to know how our political system or society will respond to today's decision overruling *Roe* and *Casey*. And even if we could foresee what will happen, we would have no authority to let that knowledge influence our decision. We can only do our job, which is to interpret the law, apply longstanding principles of *stare decisis*, and decide this case accordingly.

We therefore hold that the Constitution does not confer a right to abortion. *Roe* and *Casey* must be overruled, and the authority to regulate abortion must be returned to the people and their elected representatives.

. . .

VI

We must now decide what standard will govern if state abortion regulations undergo constitutional challenge and whether the law before us satisfies the appropriate standard.

A

Under our precedents, rational-basis review is the appropriate standard for such challenges. . . .

It follows that the States may regulate abortion for legitimate reasons, and when such regulations are challenged under the Constitution, courts cannot "substitute their social and economic beliefs for the judgment of legislative bodies." *Ferguson* [*v. Skrupa*], 372 U.S. [726,] 729–730 [(1963)]. That respect for a legislature's judgment applies even when the laws at issue concern matters of great social significance and moral substance.

A law regulating abortion, like other health and welfare laws, is entitled to a "strong presumption of validity." *Heller v. Doe*, 509 U.S. 312, [319] (1993). It must be sustained if there is a rational basis on which the legislature could have thought that it would serve legitimate state interests. *Id.*, at 320. These legitimate interests include respect for and preservation of prenatal life at all stages of development, *Gonzales* [*v.*

Carhart], 550 U.S. [124,] 157–158 [(2007)]; the protection of maternal health and safety; the elimination of particularly gruesome or barbaric medical procedures; the preservation of the integrity of the medical profession; the mitigation of fetal pain; and the prevention of discrimination on the basis of race, sex, or disability. See *id.*, at 156–157; *Roe*, 410 U.S. at 150.

B

These legitimate interests justify Mississippi's Gestational Age Act. Except "in a medical emergency or in the case of a severe fetal abnormality," the statute prohibits abortion "if the probable gestational age of the unborn human being has been determined to be greater than fifteen (15) weeks." Miss. Code Ann. § 41–41–191(4)(b). The Mississippi Legislature's findings recount the stages of "human prenatal development" and assert the State's interest in "protecting the life of the unborn." § 2(b)(i). The legislature also found that abortions performed after 15 weeks typically use the dilation and evacuation procedure, and the legislature found the use of this procedure "for nontherapeutic or elective reasons [to be] a barbaric practice, dangerous for the maternal patient, and demeaning to the medical profession." § 2(b)(i)(8); see also *Gonzales*, 550 U.S. at 135–143 (describing such procedures). These legitimate interests provide a rational basis for the Gestational Age Act, and it follows that respondents' constitutional challenge must fail.

VII

We end this opinion where we began. Abortion presents a profound moral question. The Constitution does not prohibit the citizens of each State from regulating or prohibiting abortion. *Roe* and *Casey* arrogated that authority. We now overrule those decisions and return that authority to the people and their elected representatives.

The judgment of the Fifth Circuit is reversed, and the case is remanded for further proceedings consistent with this opinion.

It is so ordered.

■ JUSTICE THOMAS, concurring.

I join the opinion of the Court because it correctly holds that there is no constitutional right to abortion. . . .

. . .

As I have previously explained, "substantive due process" is an oxymoron that "lack[s] any basis in the Constitution." *Johnson* [*v. United States*], 576 U.S. [591,] 607–608 [(2015)] (opinion of THOMAS, J.). The resolution of this case is thus straightforward. Because the Due Process Clause does not secure *any* substantive rights, it does not secure a right to abortion.

. . .

[I]n future cases, we should reconsider all of this Court's substantive due process precedents, including *Griswold* [*v. Connecticut*, 381 U.S. 479 (1965)], *Lawrence* [*v. Texas*, 539 U.S. 558 (2003)] and *Obergefell* [*v. Hodges*, 576 U.S. 644 (2015)]. . . . After overruling these demonstrably erroneous decisions, the question would remain whether other constitutional provisions guarantee the myriad rights that our substantive due process cases have generated. For example, we could consider whether any of the rights announced in this Court's substantive due process cases are "privileges or immunities of citizens of the United States" protected by the Fourteenth Amendment. Amdt. 14, § 1; see *McDonald* [*v. Chicago*], 561 U.S. [742,] 806 [(2010)] (opinion of THOMAS, J.). To answer that question, we would need to decide important antecedent questions, including whether the Privileges or Immunities Clause protects *any* rights that are not enumerated in the Constitution and, if so, how to identify those rights. See *id.*, at 854. That said, even if the Clause does protect unenumerated rights, the Court conclusively demonstrates that abortion is not one of them under any plausible interpretive approach.

. . .

■ JUSTICE KAVANAUGH, concurring.

I write separately to explain my additional views about why *Roe* [*v. Wade*, 410 U.S. 113 (1973)] was wrongly decided, why *Roe* should be overruled at this time, and the future implications of today's decision.

I

. . .

. . . The issue before this Court is what the Constitution says about abortion. The Constitution does not take sides on the issue of abortion. The text of the Constitution does not refer to or encompass abortion. To be sure, this Court has held that the Constitution protects unenumerated rights that are deeply rooted in this Nation's history and tradition, and implicit in the concept of ordered liberty. But a right to abortion is not deeply rooted in American history and tradition[.] . . .

On the question of abortion, the Constitution is therefore neither pro-life nor pro-choice. The Constitution is neutral and leaves the issue for the people and their elected representatives to resolve through the democratic process in the States or Congress—like the numerous other difficult questions of American social and economic policy that the Constitution does not address.

Because the Constitution is neutral on the issue of abortion, this Court also must be scrupulously neutral. The nine unelected Members of this Court do not possess the constitutional authority to override the democratic process and to decree either a pro-life or a pro-choice abortion policy for all 330 million people in the United States.

. . .

II

. . .

. . . I agree with the Court's application today of the principles of *stare decisis* and its conclusion that *Roe* should be overruled.

III

After today's decision, the nine Members of this Court will no longer decide the basic legality of pre-viability abortion for all 330 million Americans. That issue will be resolved by the people and their representatives in the democratic process in the States or Congress. But the parties' arguments have raised other related questions, and I address some of them here.

First is the question of how this decision will affect other precedents involving issues such as contraception and marriage—in particular, the decisions in *Griswold v. Connecticut*, 381 U.S. 479 (1965); *Eisenstadt v. Baird*, 405 U.S. 438 (1972); *Loving v. Virginia*, 388 U.S. 1 (1967); and *Obergefell v. Hodges*, 576 U.S. 644 (2015). I emphasize what the Court today states: Overruling *Roe* does *not* mean the overruling of those precedents, and does *not* threaten or cast doubt on those precedents.

Second, as I see it, some of the other abortion-related legal questions raised by today's decision are not especially difficult as a constitutional matter. For example, may a State bar a resident of that State from traveling to another State to obtain an abortion? In my view, the answer is no based on the constitutional right to interstate travel. May a State retroactively impose liability or punishment for an abortion that occurred before today's decision takes effect? In my view, the answer is no based on the Due Process Clause or the *Ex Post Facto* Clause.

Other abortion-related legal questions may emerge in the future. But this Court will no longer decide the fundamental question of whether abortion must be allowed throughout the United States through 6 weeks, or 12 weeks, or 15 weeks, or 24 weeks, or some other line. The Court will no longer decide how to evaluate the interests of the pregnant woman and the interests in protecting fetal life throughout pregnancy. Instead, those difficult moral and policy questions will be decided, as the Constitution dictates, by the people and their elected representatives through the constitutional processes of democratic self-government.

. . .

■ CHIEF JUSTICE ROBERTS, concurring in the judgment.

. . . I agree with the Court that the viability line established by *Roe* [*v. Wade*, 410 U.S. 113 (1973),] and [*Planned Parenthood of Southeastern Pa. v.*] *Casey*[, 505 U.S. 803 (1992)] should be discarded under a straightforward *stare decisis* analysis. That line never made any sense. Our abortion precedents describe the right at issue as a woman's right to choose to terminate her pregnancy. That right should therefore extend far enough to ensure a reasonable opportunity to choose, but need not extend any further—certainly not all the way to viability. Mississippi's law allows a woman three months to obtain an abortion, well beyond the point at which it is considered "late" to discover a pregnancy. See A. Ayoola, Late Recognition of Unintended Pregnancies, 32 Pub. Health Nursing 462 (2015) (pregnancy is discoverable and ordinarily discovered by six weeks of gestation). I see no sound basis for questioning the adequacy of that opportunity.

But that is all I would say, out of adherence to a simple yet fundamental principle of judicial restraint: If it is not necessary to decide more to dispose of a case, then it is necessary *not* to decide more. Perhaps we are not always perfect in following that command, and certainly there are cases that warrant an exception. But this is not one of them. Surely we should adhere closely to principles of judicial restraint here, where the broader path the Court chooses entails repudiating a constitutional right we have not only previously recognized, but also expressly reaffirmed applying the doctrine of *stare decisis*. The Court's opinion is thoughtful and thorough, but those virtues cannot compensate for the fact that its dramatic and consequential ruling is unnecessary to decide the case before us.

. . .

. . . A thoughtful Member of this Court once counseled that the difficulty of a question "admonishes us to observe the wise limitations on our function and to confine ourselves to deciding only what is necessary to the disposition of the immediate case." *Whitehouse v. Illinois Central R. Co.*, 349 U.S. 366, 372–373 (1955) (Frankfurter, J., for the Court). I would decide the question we granted review to answer—whether the previously recognized abortion right bars all abortion restrictions prior to viability, such that a ban on abortions after fifteen weeks of pregnancy is necessarily unlawful. The answer to that question is no, and there is no need to go further to decide this case.

I therefore concur only in the judgment.

■ JUSTICE BREYER, JUSTICE SOTOMAYOR, and JUSTICE KAGAN, dissenting.

. . .

. . . Yesterday, the Constitution guaranteed that a woman confronted with an unplanned pregnancy could (within reasonable limits) make her own decision about whether to bear a child, with all the life-transforming consequences that act involves. And in thus safeguarding each woman's reproductive freedom, the Constitution also protected "[t]he ability of women to participate equally in [this Nation's] economic and social life." [*Planned Parenthood of Southeastern Pa. v.*] *Casey*, 505 U.S. [803,] 856 [(1992)]. But no longer. As of today, this Court holds, a State can always force a woman to give birth, prohibiting even the earliest abortions. A State can thus transform what, when freely undertaken, is a wonder into what, when forced, may be a nightmare. . . . The Constitution will, today's majority holds, provide no shield, despite its guarantees of liberty and equality for all.

And no one should be confident that this majority is done with its work. The right *Roe* [*v. Wade*, 410 U.S. 113 (1973)] and *Casey* recognized does not stand alone. To the contrary, the Court has linked it for decades to other settled freedoms involving bodily integrity, familial relationships, and procreation. Most obviously, the right to terminate a pregnancy arose straight out of the right to purchase and use contraception. See *Griswold v. Connecticut*, 381 U.S. 479 (1965); *Eisenstadt v. Baird*, 405 U.S. 438 (1972). In turn, those rights led, more recently, to rights of same-sex intimacy and marriage. See *Lawrence v. Texas*, 539 U.S. 558 (2003); *Obergefell v. Hodges*, 576 U.S. 644 (2015). They are all part of the same constitutional fabric[.] . . . The majority (or to be more accurate, most of it) is eager to tell us today that nothing it does "cast[s] doubt on precedents that do not concern abortion." *Ante*, at ___; cf. *ante*, at ___ (THOMAS, J., concurring) (advocating the overruling of *Griswold*, *Lawrence*, and *Obergefell*). But how could that be? The lone rationale for what the majority does today is that the right to elect an abortion is not "deeply rooted in history": Not until *Roe*, the majority argues, did people think abortion fell within the Constitution's guarantee of liberty. The same could be said, though, of most of the rights the majority claims it is not tampering with. . . . So one of two things must be true. Either the majority does not really believe in its own reasoning. Or if it does, all rights that have no history stretching back to the mid-19th century are insecure. Either the mass of the majority's opinion is hypocrisy, or additional constitutional rights are under threat. It is one or the other.

One piece of evidence on that score seems especially salient: The majority's cavalier approach to overturning this Court's precedents. *Stare decisis*[,] . . . a foundation stone of the rule of law[,] . . . is a doctrine of judicial modesty and humility. . . . The majority has no good reason for the upheaval in law and society it sets off. *Roe* and *Casey* have been the law of the land for decades[.] . . . Women have relied on the availability of abortion both in structuring their relationships and in planning their lives. The legal framework *Roe* and *Casey* developed to balance the competing interests in this sphere has proved workable in courts across the country. No recent developments, in either law or fact, have eroded or cast doubt on those precedents. Nothing, in short, has changed. . . . The Court reverses course today for one reason and one reason only: because the composition of this Court has changed. . . . Today, the proclivities of individuals rule. The Court departs from its obligation to faithfully and impartially apply the law. We dissent.

I

. . . To hear the majority tell the tale, *Roe* and *Casey* are aberrations: They came from nowhere, went nowhere—and so are easy to excise from this Nation's constitutional law. That is not true. . . . *Roe* and *Casey* were from the beginning, and are even more now, embedded in core constitutional concepts of individual freedom, and of the equal rights of citizens to decide on the shape of their lives. . . . [I]n this Nation, we do not believe that a government controlling all private choices is compatible with a free people. . . . We believe in a Constitution that puts some issues off limits to majority rule. Even in the face of public opposition, we uphold the right of individuals—yes, including women—to make their own choices and chart their own futures. Or at least, we did once.

A

. . . *Roe* struck down a state law making it a crime to perform an abortion unless its purpose was to save a woman's life. The *Roe* Court knew it was treading on difficult and disputed ground. . . . But by a 7-to-2 vote, the Court held that in the earlier stages of pregnancy, [the] . . . contested and contestable [abortion] choice must belong to a woman, in consultation with her family and doctor. The Court explained that a long line of precedents, "founded in the Fourteenth Amendment's concept of personal liberty," protected individual decisionmaking related to "marriage, procreation, contraception, family relationships, and child rearing and education." *Id.*, at 152–153 (citations omitted). For the same reasons, the Court held, the Constitution must protect "a woman's decision whether or not to terminate her pregnancy." *Id.*, at 153. The Court recognized the myriad ways bearing a child can alter the "life and future" of a woman and other members of her family. *Ibid.* A State could not, "by adopting one theory of life," override all "rights of the pregnant woman." *Id.*, at 162.

At the same time, . . . the Court recognized "valid interest[s]" of the State "in regulating the abortion decision." *Id.*, at 153. The Court noted in particular "important interests" in "protecting potential life," "maintaining medical standards," and "safeguarding [the] health" of the woman. *Id.*, at 154. No "absolut[ist]" account of the woman's right could wipe away those significant state claims. *Ibid.*

The Court therefore struck a balance, turning on the stage of the pregnancy at which the abortion would occur. . . .

In the 20 years between *Roe* and *Casey*, the Court expressly reaffirmed *Roe* on two occasions, and applied it on many more. . . .

Then, in *Casey*, the Court considered the matter anew, and again upheld *Roe*'s core precepts. *Casey* is in significant measure a precedent about the doctrine of precedent[.] . . . The key thing now is the substantive aspect of the Court's considered conclusion that "the essential holding of *Roe v. Wade* should be retained and once again reaffirmed." 505 U.S. at 846.

Central to that conclusion was a full-throated restatement of a woman's right to choose. Like *Roe*, *Casey* grounded that right in the Fourteenth Amendment's guarantee of "liberty." That guarantee encompasses realms of conduct not specifically referenced in the Constitution: "Marriage is mentioned nowhere" in that document, yet the Court was "no doubt correct" to protect the freedom to marry "against state interference." 505 U.S. at 847–848. And the guarantee of liberty encompasses conduct today that was not protected at the time of the Fourteenth Amendment. See *id.*, at 848. "It is settled now," the Court said[,] . . . that "the Constitution places limits on a State's right to interfere with a person's most basic decisions about family and parenthood, as well as bodily integrity." *Id.*, at 849 (citations omitted). Especially important in this web of precedents protecting an individual's most "personal choices" were those guaranteeing the right to contraception. *Ibid.*; see *id.*, at 852–853. In those cases, the Court had recognized "the right of the individual" to make the vastly consequential "decision whether to bear" a child. *Id.*, at 851 (emphasis deleted). So too, *Casey* reasoned, the liberty clause protects the decision of a woman confronting an unplanned pregnancy. Her decision about abortion was central, in the same way, to her capacity to chart her life's course. See *id.*, at 853.

In reaffirming the right *Roe* recognized, the Court took full account of the diversity of views on abortion, and the importance of various competing state interests. . . .

So *Casey* again struck a balance, differing from *Roe*'s in only incremental ways. It retained *Roe*'s "central holding" that the State could bar abortion only after viability. 505 U.S. at 860 (majority opinion). The viability line, *Casey* thought, was "more workable" than any other in marking the place where the woman's liberty interest gave way to a State's efforts to preserve potential life. *Id.*, at 870 (plurality opinion). At that point, a "second life" was capable of "independent existence." *Ibid.* If the woman even by then had not acted, she lacked adequate grounds to object to "the State's intervention on [the developing child's] behalf." *Ibid.* At the same time, *Casey* decided, based on two decades of experience, that the *Roe* framework did not give States sufficient ability to regulate abortion prior to viability. In that period, . . . the State could regulate not only to protect the woman's health but also to "promot[e] prenatal life." 505 U.S. at 873 (plurality opinion). In particular, the State could ensure informed choice and could try to promote childbirth. See *id.*, at 877–878. But the State still could not place an "undue burden"—or "substantial obstacle"—"in the path of a woman seeking an abortion." *Id.*, at 878. Prior to viability, the woman, consistent with the constitutional "meaning of liberty," must "retain the ultimate control over her destiny and her body." *Id.*, at 869.

. . . *Roe* and *Casey* invoked powerful state interests in that protection, operative at every stage of the pregnancy and overriding the woman's liberty after viability. The strength of those state interests is exactly why the Court allowed greater restrictions on the abortion right than on other rights deriving from the Fourteenth Amendment. But what

Roe and *Casey* also recognized—which today's majority does not—is that a woman's freedom and equality are likewise involved. That fact—the presence of countervailing interests—is what made the abortion question hard, and what necessitated balancing. . . . To the majority "balance" is a dirty word, as moderation is a foreign concept. The majority would allow States to ban abortion from conception onward because it does not think forced childbirth at all implicates a woman's rights to equality and freedom. . . . The constitutional regime we have lived in for the last 50 years recognized competing interests, and sought a balance between them. The constitutional regime we enter today erases the woman's interest and recognizes only the State's (or the Federal Government's).

B

. . .

The majority's core legal postulate . . . is that we in the 21st century must read the Fourteenth Amendment just as its ratifiers did. And that is indeed what the majority emphasizes over and over again. If the ratifiers did not understand something as central to freedom, then neither can we. Or said more particularly: If those people did not understand reproductive rights as part of the guarantee of liberty conferred in the Fourteenth Amendment, then those rights do not exist.

. . . [N]ote a mistake in the just preceding sentence. We referred there to the "people" who ratified the Fourteenth Amendment: What rights did those "people" have in their heads at the time? But, of course, "people" did not ratify the Fourteenth Amendment. Men did. So it is perhaps not so surprising that the ratifiers were not perfectly attuned to the importance of reproductive rights for women's liberty, or for their capacity to participate as equal members of our Nation. Indeed, the ratifiers—both in 1868 and when the original Constitution was approved in 1788—did not understand women as full members of the community embraced by the phrase "We the People." . . . Those responsible for the original Constitution, including the Fourteenth Amendment, did not perceive women as equals, and did not recognize women's rights. When the majority says that we must read our foundational charter as viewed at the time of ratification . . ., it consigns women to second-class citizenship.

. . .

. . . [T]his Court has rejected the majority's pinched view of how to read our Constitution. . . . The Framers (both in 1788 and 1868) understood that the world changes. So they did not define rights by reference to the specific practices existing at the time. Instead, the Framers defined rights in general terms, to permit future evolution in their scope and meaning. And over the course of our history, this Court has taken up the Framers' invitation. It has kept true to the Framers' principles by applying them in new ways, responsive to new societal understandings and conditions.

Nowhere has that approach been more prevalent than in construing the majestic but open-ended words of the Fourteenth Amendment—the guarantees of "liberty" and "equality" for all. . . .

That does not mean anything goes. . . . [A]pplications of liberty and equality can evolve while remaining grounded in constitutional principles, constitutional history, and constitutional precedents. . . .

All that is what *Casey* understood. *Casey* explicitly rejected the present majority's method. To hold otherwise—as the majority does today—"would be inconsistent with our law." 505 U.S. at 847. Why? Because the Court has "vindicated [the] principle" over and over that (no matter the sentiment in 1868) "there is a realm of personal liberty which the government may not enter"—especially relating to "bodily integrity" and "family life." *Id.*, at 847, 849, 851 . . .

. . .

Casey similarly recognized the need to extend the constitutional sphere of liberty to a previously excluded group. The Court then understood, as the majority today does not, that the men who ratified the Fourteenth Amendment and wrote the state laws of the time did not view women as full and equal citizens. A woman then, *Casey* wrote, "had no legal existence separate from her husband." 505 U.S. at 897. Women were seen only "as the center of home and family life," without "full and independent legal status under the Constitution." *Ibid.* But that could not be true any longer: The State could not now insist on the historically dominant "vision of the woman's role." *Id.*, at 852. And equal citizenship, *Casey* realized, was inescapably connected to reproductive rights. "The ability of women to participate equally" in the "life of the Nation"—in all its economic, social, political, and legal aspects—"has been facilitated by their ability to control their reproductive lives." *Id.*, at 856. Without the ability to decide whether and when to have children, women could not—in the way men took for granted—determine how they would live their lives, and how they would contribute to the society around them.

. . .

Faced with all these connections between *Roe/Casey* and judicial decisions recognizing other constitutional rights, the majority tells everyone not to worry. It can (so it says) neatly extract the right to choose from the constitutional edifice without affecting any associated rights. . . . Should the audience for these too-much-repeated protestations be duly satisfied? We think not.

. . .

As a matter of constitutional substance, the majority's opinion has all the flaws its method would suggest. Because laws in 1868 deprived women of any control over their bodies, the majority approves States doing so today. Because those laws prevented women from charting the course of their own lives, the majority says States can do the same again. Because in 1868, the government could tell a pregnant woman—even in the first days of her pregnancy—that she could do nothing but bear a child, it can once more impose that command. Today's decision strips women of agency over what even the majority agrees is a contested and contestable moral issue. It forces her to carry out the State's will, whatever the circumstances and whatever the harm it will wreak on her and her family. In the Fourteenth Amendment's terms, it takes away her liberty. Even before we get to *stare decisis*, we dissent.

II

By overruling *Roe*, *Casey*, and more than 20 cases reaffirming or applying the constitutional right to abortion, the majority abandons *stare decisis*, a principle central to the rule of law. . . .

. . .

In any event "[w]hether or not we . . . agree" with a prior precedent is the beginning, not the end, of our analysis—and the remaining "principles of *stare decisis* weigh heavily against overruling" *Roe* and *Casey*. *Dickerson v. United States*, 530 U.S. 428, 443 (2000). *Casey* itself applied those principles, in one of this Court's most important precedents about precedent. After assessing the traditional *stare decisis* factors, *Casey* reached the only conclusion possible—that *stare decisis* operates powerfully here. It still does. The standards *Roe* and *Casey* set out are perfectly workable. No changes in either law or fact have eroded the two decisions. And tens of millions of American women have relied, and continue to rely, on the right to choose. So under traditional *stare decisis* principles, the majority has no special justification for the harm it causes.

. . .

A

Contrary to the majority's view, there is nothing unworkable about *Casey*'s "undue burden" standard. Its primary focus on whether a State has placed a "substantial obstacle" on a woman seeking an abortion is "the sort of inquiry familiar to judges across a variety of contexts." *June Medical Services L.L.C. v. Russo*, 591 U.S. ___, ___, 140 S.Ct. 2103 (2020) (ROBERTS, C. J., concurring in judgment). And it has given rise to no more conflict in application than many standards this Court and others unhesitatingly apply every day.

. . .

And the undue burden standard has given rise to no unusual difficulties. Of course, it has provoked some disagreement among judges. *Casey* knew it would: That much "is to be expected in the application of any legal standard which must accommodate life's complexity." 505 U.S. at 878 (plurality opinion). Which is to say: That much is to be expected in the application of any legal standard. . . .

Anyone concerned about workability should consider the majority's substitute standard. The majority says a law regulating or banning abortion "must be sustained if there is a rational basis on which the legislature could have thought that it would serve legitimate state interests." *Ante,* at ___. And the majority lists interests like "respect for and preservation of prenatal life," "protection of maternal health," elimination of certain "medical procedures," "mitigation of fetal pain," and others. *Ante,* at ___. This Court will surely face critical questions about how that test applies. Must a state law allow abortions when necessary to protect a woman's life and health? And if so, exactly when? How much risk to a woman's life can a State force her to incur, before the Fourteenth Amendment's protection of life kicks in? Suppose a patient with pulmonary hypertension has a 30-to-50 percent risk of dying with ongoing pregnancy; is that enough? And short of death, how much illness or injury can the State require her to accept, consistent with the Amendment's protection of liberty and equality? Further, the Court may face questions about the application of abortion regulations to medical care most people view as quite different from abortion. What about the morning-after pill? IUDs? In vitro fertilization? And how about the use of dilation and evacuation or medication for miscarriage management? See generally L. Harris, Navigating Loss of Abortion Services—A Large Academic Medical Center Prepares for the Overturn of *Roe v. Wade,* 386 New England J. Med. 2061 (2022).[12]

. . .

B

When overruling constitutional precedent, the Court has almost always pointed to major legal or factual changes undermining a decision's original basis. . . . In the end, the majority throws longstanding precedent to the winds without showing that anything significant has changed to justify its radical reshaping of the law.

1

Subsequent legal developments have only reinforced *Roe* and *Casey.* The Court has continued to embrace all the decisions *Roe* and *Casey* cited, decisions which recognize a constitutional right for an individual to make her own choices about "intimate relationships, the family," and contraception. *Casey,* 505 U.S. at 857. *Roe* and *Casey* have themselves formed the legal foundation for subsequent decisions protecting these profoundly personal choices. . . . *Roe* and *Casey* are inextricably interwoven with decades of precedent about the meaning of the Fourteenth Amendment. While the majority might wish it otherwise, *Roe* and *Casey* are the very opposite of " 'obsolete constitutional thinking.' " *Agostini v. Felton,* 521 U.S. 203, 236 (1997) (quoting *Casey,* 505 U.S. at 857).

---

[12] To take just the last, most medical treatments for miscarriage are identical to those used in abortions. Blanket restrictions on "abortion" procedures and medications therefore may be understood to deprive women of effective treatment for miscarriages, which occur in about 10 to 30 percent of pregnancies.

Moreover, no subsequent factual developments have undermined *Roe* and *Casey*. . .

. . . The majority briefly notes the growing prevalence of safe haven laws and demand for adoption, but, to the degree that these are changes at all, they too are irrelevant. Neither reduces the health risks or financial costs of going through pregnancy and childbirth. Moreover, the choice to give up parental rights after giving birth is altogether different from the choice not to carry a pregnancy to term. The reality is that few women denied an abortion will choose adoption. The vast majority will continue, just as in *Roe* and *Casey*'s time, to shoulder the costs of childrearing. Whether or not they choose to parent, they will experience the profound loss of autonomy and dignity that coerced pregnancy and birth always impose.

Mississippi's own record illustrates how little facts on the ground have changed since *Roe* and *Casey*, notwithstanding the majority's supposed "modern developments." Sixty-two percent of pregnancies in Mississippi are unplanned, yet Mississippi does not require insurance to cover contraceptives and prohibits educators from demonstrating proper contraceptive use. The State neither bans pregnancy discrimination nor requires provision of paid parental leave. It has strict eligibility requirements for Medicaid and nutrition assistance, leaving many women and families without basic medical care or enough food. Although 86 percent of pregnancy-related deaths in the State are due to postpartum complications, Mississippi rejected federal funding to provide a year's worth of Medicaid coverage to women after giving birth. Perhaps unsurprisingly, health outcomes in Mississippi are abysmal for both women and children. Mississippi has the highest infant mortality rate in the country, and some of the highest rates for preterm birth, low birthweight, cesarean section, and maternal death. It is approximately 75 times more dangerous for a woman in the State to carry a pregnancy to term than to have an abortion. We do not say that every State is Mississippi, and we are sure some have made gains since *Roe* and *Casey* in providing support for women and children. But a state-by-state analysis by public health professionals shows that States with the most restrictive abortion policies also continue to invest the least in women's and children's health.

. . .

C

The reasons for retaining *Roe* and *Casey* gain further strength from the overwhelming reliance interests those decisions have created. The Court adheres to precedent not just for institutional reasons, but because it recognizes that stability in the law is "an essential thread in the mantle of protection that the law affords the individual." *Florida Dept. of Health and Rehabilitative Servs. v. Florida Nursing Home Assn.*, 450 U.S. 147 (1981) (Stevens, J., concurring). So when overruling precedent "would dislodge [individuals'] settled rights and expectations," *stare decisis* has "added force." *Hilton v. South Carolina Public Railways Comm'n*, 502 U.S. 197, 202 (1991). *Casey* understood that to deny individuals' reliance on *Roe* was to "refuse to face the fact[s]." 505 U.S. at 856. Today the majority refuses to face the facts. "The most striking feature of the [majority] is the absence of any serious discussion" of how its ruling will affect women. By characterizing *Casey*'s reliance arguments as "generalized assertions about the national psyche," *ante*, at ___, it reveals how little it knows or cares about women's lives or about the suffering its decision will cause.

. . .

The disruption of overturning *Roe* and *Casey* will . . . be profound. Abortion is a common medical procedure and a familiar experience in women's lives. About 18 percent of pregnancies in this country end in abortion, and about one quarter of American women will have an abortion before the age of 45. Those numbers reflect the predictable and life-changing effects of carrying a pregnancy, giving birth, and becoming a parent. As *Casey* understood, people today rely on their ability to control and time pregnancies when making countless life decisions: where to live, whether and how to invest in education or careers, how to allocate financial resources, and how to approach intimate and family relationships. Women may count on abortion access for when contraception fails. They may count on abortion access for when contraception cannot be used, for example, if they were raped. They may count on abortion for when something changes in the midst of a pregnancy, whether it involves family or financial circumstances, unanticipated medical complications, or heartbreaking fetal diagnoses. Taking away the right to abortion, as the majority does today, destroys all those individual plans and expectations. In so doing, it diminishes women's opportunities to participate fully and equally in the Nation's political, social, and economic life. See Brief for Economists as *Amici Curiae* 13 (showing that abortion availability has "large effects on women's education, labor force participation, occupations, and earnings" (footnotes omitted)).

The majority's response to these obvious points exists far from the reality American women actually live. The majority proclaims that " 'reproductive planning could take virtually immediate account of any sudden restoration of state authority to ban abortions.' " The facts are: 45 percent of pregnancies in the United States are unplanned. Even the most effective contraceptives fail, and effective contraceptives are not universally accessible.[24] Not all sexual activity is consensual and not all contraceptive choices are made by the party who risks pregnancy. The Mississippi law at issue here, for example, has no exception for rape or

---

[24] See Brief for 547 Deans 6–7 (noting that 51 percent of women who terminated their pregnancies reported using contraceptives during the month in which they conceived); Brief for Lawyers' Committee for Civil Rights Under Law et al. as *Amici Curiae* 12–14 (explaining financial and geographic barriers to access to effective contraceptives).

incest, even for underage women. Finally, the majority ignores . . . that some women decide to have an abortion because their circumstances change during a pregnancy. Human bodies care little for hopes and plans. Events can occur after conception, from unexpected medical risks to changes in family circumstances, which profoundly alter what it means to carry a pregnancy to term. In all these situations, women have expected that they will get to decide, perhaps in consultation with their families or doctors but free from state interference, whether to continue a pregnancy. For those who will now have to undergo that pregnancy, the loss of *Roe* and *Casey* could be disastrous.

That is especially so for women without money. When we "count[ ] the cost of [*Roe's*] repudiation" on women who once relied on that decision, it is not hard to see where the greatest burden will fall. *Casey*, 505 U.S. at 855. In States that bar abortion, women of means will still be able to travel to obtain the services they need.[25] It is women who cannot afford to do so who will suffer most. These are the women most likely to seek abortion care in the first place. Women living below the federal poverty line experience unintended pregnancies at rates five times higher than higher income women do, and nearly half of women who seek abortion care live in households below the poverty line. Even with *Roe's* protection, these women face immense obstacles to raising the money needed to obtain abortion care early in their pregnancy.[26] After today, in States where legal abortions are not available, they will lose any ability to obtain safe, legal abortion care. They will not have the money to make the trip necessary; or to obtain childcare for that time; or to take time off work. Many will endure the costs and risks of pregnancy and giving birth against their wishes. Others will turn in desperation to illegal and unsafe abortions. They may lose not just their freedom, but their lives.[27]

Finally, the expectation of reproductive control is integral to many women's identity and their place in the Nation. That expectation helps define a woman as an "equal citizen[ ]," with all the rights, privileges, and obligations that status entails. *Gonzales* [*v. Carhart*, 550 U.S. [124,] 172 [(2007)] (Ginsburg, J., dissenting)]. It reflects that she is an autonomous person, and that society and the law recognize her as such.

---

[25] Even assuming that [states are not successful in preventing interstate travel to obtain an abortion] . . ., increased out-of-state demand will lead to longer wait times and decreased availability of service in States still providing abortions. . . .

[26] The average cost of a first-trimester abortion is about $500. Federal insurance generally does not cover the cost of abortion, and 35 percent of American adults do not have cash on hand to cover an unexpected expense that high.

[27] Mississippi is likely to be one of the States where these costs are highest, though history shows that it will have company. . . . Mississippi provides only the barest financial support to pregnant women. The State will greatly restrict abortion care without addressing any of the financial, health, and family needs that motivate many women to seek it. The effects will be felt most severely, as they always have been, on the bodies of the poor. The history of state abortion restrictions is a history of heavy costs exacted from the most vulnerable women. It is a history of women seeking illegal abortions in hotel rooms and home kitchens; of women trying to self-induce abortions by douching with bleach, injecting lye, and penetrating themselves with knitting needles, scissors, and coat hangers. See L. Reagan, When Abortion Was a Crime 42–43, 198–199, 208–209 (1997). It is a history of women dying.

Like many constitutional rights, the right to choose situates a woman in relationship to others and to the government. It helps define a sphere of freedom, in which a person has the capacity to make choices free of government control. As *Casey* recognized, the right "order[s]" her "thinking" as well as her "living." 505 U.S. at 856. Beyond any individual choice about residence, or education, or career, her whole life reflects the control and authority that the right grants.

Withdrawing a woman's right to choose whether to continue a pregnancy does not mean that no choice is being made. It means that a majority of today's Court has wrenched this choice from women and given it to the States. To allow a State to exert control over one of "the most intimate and personal choices" a woman may make is not only to affect the course of her life, monumental as those effects might be. *Id.*, at 851. It is to alter her "views of [herself]" and her understanding of her "place[ ] in society" as someone with the recognized dignity and authority to make these choices. *Id.*, at 856. Women have relied on *Roe* and *Casey* in this way for 50 years. Many have never known anything else. When *Roe* and *Casey* disappear, the loss of power, control, and dignity will be immense.

. . .

The majority claims that the reliance interests women have in *Roe* and *Casey* are too "intangible" for the Court to consider, even if it were inclined to do so. This is to ignore as judges what we know as men and women. The interests women have in *Roe* and *Casey* are perfectly, viscerally concrete. Countless women will now make different decisions about careers, education, relationships, and whether to try to become pregnant than they would have when *Roe* served as a backstop. Other women will carry pregnancies to term, with all the costs and risk of harm that involves, when they would previously have chosen to obtain an abortion. For millions of women, *Roe* and *Casey* have been critical in giving them control of their bodies and their lives. Closing our eyes to the suffering today's decision will impose will not make that suffering disappear. The majority cannot escape its obligation to "count[ ] the cost[s]" of its decision by invoking the "conflicting arguments" of "contending sides." *Casey*, 505 U.S. at 855. *Stare decisis* requires that the Court calculate the costs of a decision's repudiation on those who have relied on the decision, not on those who have disavowed it.

More broadly, the majority's approach to reliance cannot be reconciled with our Nation's understanding of constitutional rights. The majority's insistence on a "concrete," economic showing would preclude a finding of reliance on a wide variety of decisions recognizing constitutional rights—such as the right to express opinions, or choose whom to marry, or decide how to educate children. The Court, on the majority's logic, could transfer those choices to the State without having to consider a person's settled understanding that the law makes them hers. That must be wrong. All those rights, like the right to obtain an abortion, profoundly affect and, indeed, anchor individual lives. To recognize that people have relied on these rights is not to dabble in abstractions, but to acknowledge some of the most "concrete" and familiar aspects of human life and liberty.

All those rights, like the one here, also have a societal dimension, because of the role constitutional liberties play in our structure of government. Rescinding an individual right in its entirety and conferring it on the State, an action the Court takes today for the first time in history, affects all who have relied on our constitutional system of government and its structure of individual liberties protected from state oversight. *Roe* and *Casey* have of course aroused controversy and provoked disagreement. But the right those decisions conferred and reaffirmed is part of society's understanding of constitutional law and of how the Court has defined the liberty and equality that women are entitled to claim.

After today, young women will come of age with fewer rights than their mothers and grandmothers had. The majority accomplishes that result without so much as considering how women have relied on the right to choose or what it means to take that right away. The majority's refusal even to consider the life-altering consequences of reversing *Roe* and *Casey* is a stunning indictment of its decision.

D

One last consideration counsels against the majority's ruling: the very controversy surrounding *Roe* and *Casey*. The majority accuses *Casey* of acting outside the bounds of the law to quell the conflict over abortion—of imposing an unprincipled "settlement" of the issue in an effort to end "national division." But that is not what *Casey* did. As shown above, *Casey* applied traditional principles of *stare decisis*—which the majority today ignores—in reaffirming *Roe*. *Casey* carefully assessed changed circumstances (none) and reliance interests (profound). It considered every aspect of how *Roe*'s framework operated. It adhered to the law in its analysis, and it reached the conclusion that the law required. True enough that *Casey* took notice of the "national controversy" about abortion: The Court knew in 1992, as it did in 1973, that abortion was a "divisive issue." *Casey*, 505 U.S. at 867–868; see *Roe*, 410 U.S. at 116. But *Casey*'s reason for acknowledging public conflict was the exact opposite of what the majority insinuates. *Casey* addressed the national controversy in order to emphasize how important it was, in that case of all cases, for the Court to stick to the law. Would that today's majority had done likewise.

Consider how the majority itself summarizes this aspect of *Casey*:

"The American people's belief in the rule of law would be shaken if they lost respect for this Court as an institution that decides important cases based on principle, not 'social and political pressures.' There is a special danger that the public will perceive a decision as having been made for unprincipled reasons when the Court overrules a controversial 'watershed' decision, such as *Roe*. A decision overruling *Roe* would be perceived as having been made 'under fire' and as a 'surrender to political pressure.' " *Ante*, at ___–___ (citations omitted).

That seems to us a good description. And it seems to us right. The majority responds (if we understand it correctly): well, yes, but we have to apply the law. To which *Casey* would have said: That is exactly the point. Here, more than anywhere, the Court needs to apply the law—particularly the law of *stare decisis*. Here, we know that citizens will continue to contest the Court's decision, because "[m]en and women of good conscience" deeply disagree about abortion. *Casey*, 505 U.S. at 850. When that contestation takes place—but when there is no legal basis for reversing course—the Court needs to be steadfast, to stand its ground. That is what the rule of law requires. And that is what respect for this Court depends on.

"The promise of constancy, once given" in so charged an environment, *Casey* explained, "binds its maker for as long as" the "understanding of the issue has not changed so fundamentally as to render the commitment obsolete." *Id.*, at 868. A breach of that promise is "nothing less than a breach of faith." *Ibid.* "[A]nd no Court that broke its faith with the people could sensibly expect credit for principle." *Ibid.* No Court breaking its faith in that way would *deserve* credit for principle. As one of *Casey*'s authors wrote in another case, "Our legitimacy requires, above all, that we adhere to *stare decisis*" in "sensitive political contexts" where "partisan controversy abounds." *Bush v. Vera*, 517 U.S. 952, 985 (1996) (opinion of O'Connor, J.).

Justice Jackson once called a decision he dissented from a "loaded weapon," ready to hand for improper uses. *Korematsu v. United States*, 323 U.S. 214, 246 (1944). We fear that today's decision, departing from *stare decisis* for no legitimate reason, is its own loaded weapon. Weakening *stare decisis* threatens to upend bedrock legal doctrines, far beyond any single decision. Weakening *stare decisis* creates profound legal instability. And as *Casey* recognized, weakening *stare decisis* in a hotly contested case like this one calls into question this Court's commitment to legal principle. It makes the Court appear not restrained but aggressive, not modest but grasping. In all those ways, today's decision takes aim, we fear, at the rule of law.

III

"Power, not reason, is the new currency of this Court's decisionmaking." *Payne* [*v. Tennessee*, 501 U.S. 808, 844 (1991)] (Marshall, J., dissenting). *Roe* has stood for fifty years. *Casey*, a precedent about precedent specifically confirming *Roe*, has stood for thirty. And the doctrine of *stare decisis*—a critical element of the rule of law—stands foursquare behind their continued existence. The right those decisions established and preserved is embedded in our constitutional law, both originating in and leading to other rights protecting bodily integrity, personal autonomy, and family relationships. The abortion right is also embedded in the lives of women—shaping their expectations, influencing their choices about relationships and work, supporting (as all reproductive rights do) their social and economic equality. Since the right's recognition (and affirmation), nothing has changed to support what the majority does today. Neither law nor facts nor attitudes have provided any new reasons to reach a different result than *Roe* and *Casey* did. All that has changed is this Court.

. . .

With sorrow—for this Court, but more, for the many millions of American women who have today lost a fundamental constitutional protection—we dissent.

NOTES

1. Justice Samuel Alito's majority opinion insists that *Dobbs* is only a ruling on abortion and nothing else, claiming abortion is unique. Do you think this view will prevail at least in the shorter term at the Supreme Court, given Justice Brett Kavanaugh's concurrence and assuming no changes in Court membership? How about in the longer term? Will the line-drawing in Alito's and Kavanaugh's opinions hold across time, do you think? Or are the Supreme Court's privacy rulings in cases like *Griswold v. Connecticut* and *Eisenstadt v. Baird*, along with its liberty-based rulings in cases like *Lawrence v. Texas* and *Obergefell v. Hodges* now in serious peril, as the reasoning of Alito's opinion, as elaborated by Justice Clarence Thomas's concurrence and challenged by the joint dissent, suggests? Might *Dobbs'* emphasis on *Roe* not simply being wrong but "egregiously wrong" serve as a way to hold the line at *Dobbs*?

2. What does *Dobbs* mean for the Fourteenth Amendment equal protection rights that cisheterosexual women presently enjoy? *Dobbs* itself rejects Fourteenth Amendment sex equality defenses of *Roe*, *Casey*, and the abortion right they protect. Does this suggest to you that constitutional sex equality rights are secure in their present form after *Dobbs*? Or does *Dobbs'* particular way of distinguishing them—focusing on women's biological differences from men—suggest to you prospects for their future constriction? Could *Dobbs* in other ways lay the foundation for the roll-back of constitutional sex equality guarantees? For perspective, see the account of the *Dobbs* draft opinion offered in Marc Spindelman, *What 'Dobbs' Means for Women's Equality (The Seeds of Unraveling a Host of Gender-based Protections are Present in the Draft Opinion)*, THE AM. PROSPECT (June 20, 2022), https://prospect.org/justice/what-dobbs-means-for-womens-equality/.

3. What other family law impacts might *Dobbs* have that you can already see?

CHAPTER 4

PARENTING

A. PARENTAL AUTHORITY AND ITS LIMITS

1. EDUCATION

On page 368 of the Unabridged 7th edition, and on page 276 of the Concise 7th edition, after note 4, add the following note:

5. A public school's regulation of a minor student's off-campus speech may intrude on a parent's authority to make childrearing decisions. In *Manahoy Area School District v. B.L.*, 141 S.Ct. 2038 (2021), the Court held that a public high school violated a student's First Amendment rights when it suspended her from the cheerleading team after she posted vulgar language and gestures criticizing the school and the team on social media while away from the school and outside of school hours. In distinguishing the school's efforts to regulate off-campus speech as compared to on-campus speech, the Court explained that:

> [A] school, in relation to off-campus speech, will rarely stand *in loco parentis*. The doctrine of *in loco parentis* treats school administrators as standing in the place of students' parents under circumstances where the children's actual parents cannot protect, guide, and discipline them. Geographically speaking, off-campus speech will normally fall within the zone of parental, rather than school-related, responsibility.

Id. at 2046. The school argued that it had "an interest in prohibiting students from using vulgar language to criticize a school team or its coaches—at least when that criticism might well be transmitted to other students, team members, coaches, and faculty." *Id.* at 2047. In considering "the school's interest in teaching good manners and consequently in punishing the use of vulgar language aimed at part of the school community", the Court found that the school's "anti-vulgarity interest is weakened considerably by the fact that B. L. spoke outside the school on her own time" and that she "spoke under circumstances where the school did not stand *in loco parentis.*" *Id.* The Court expressly noted that "there is no reason to believe B. L.'s parents had delegated to school officials their own control of B. L.'s behavior" when she was off campus. *Id.*

4. CHILD NEGLECT AND ABUSE

On page 382 of the Unabridged 7th edition, after note 3, and on page 283 of the Concise 7th edition, after note 2, add the following:

A number of scholars and advocates argue that the child welfare system cannot be reformed and must be abolished instead. Consider this excerpt by Professor Dorothy Roberts, a leading thinker in the movement to abolish the current child welfare system:

The uprisings taking place across the nation and the world have brought unprecedented attention to abolition as a political vision and organizing strategy. More Americans are recognizing that police killings of black people are so pervasive that they can no longer be considered aberrations. Rather, police violence stems from the very function of policing to enforce an unjust racial order.

Policing, therefore, cannot be fixed by more failed reforms; it must be abolished. The most prominent demand emerging from the protests is to defund the police and reallocate the money to provide health care, education, jobs with living wages, and affordable housing.

I am inspired by calls to defund the police. But I am concerned by recommendations to transfer money, resources and authority from the police to health and human services agencies that handle child protective services (CPS). These proposals ignore how the misnamed "child welfare" system, like the misnamed "criminal justice" system, is designed to regulate and punish black and other marginalized people. It could be more accurately referred to as the "family regulation system."

. . .

These recommendations reflect a more general failure to understand CPS as an integral part of the U.S. carceral regime. Regulating and destroying black, brown and indigenous families in the name of child protection has been essential to the "ongoing white supremacist nation building project" as much as prisons and police. Like the prison industrial complex, the foster industrial complex is a multi-billion-dollar government apparatus that regulates millions of marginalized people through intrusive investigations, monitoring and forcible removal of children from their homes to be placed in foster care, group homes and "therapeutic" detention facilities.

The vast majority of child welfare investigations and removals involve allegations of neglect related to poverty, and black families are targeted the most for state disruption. Just as police don't make communities safe, CPS affirmatively harms children and their families while failing to address the structural causes for their hardships. Residents of black neighborhoods live in fear of state agents entering their homes, interrogating them, and taking their children as much as they fear police harassing them in the streets.

Almost 20 years ago, I wrote a book about anti-black racism in the family regulation system—*Shattered Bonds: The Color of Child Welfare*. Since then, "racial disproportionality" has become a buzzword in child welfare research and policymaking. Despite numerous reforms, the system has not changed its punitive ideology or racist impact. The foster industrial complex can't be fixed; it must be abolished.

. . .

There is a small but growing movement to radically transform or abolish the family regulation system, ignited by black mothers who have been separated from their children and joined by former foster youth, social justice activists, legal services providers, nonprofit organizations, and scholars. Our goal is not only to dismantle the current system, but also to imagine and create better ways of caring for children, meeting families' needs, and preventing domestic violence. Like demands to defund police, foster care abolition includes diverting the billions of dollars spent on separating children from their families to cash assistance, health care, housing and other material supports provided directly and non-coercively to parents and other family caregivers and care networks.

Ultimately, these abolitionist movements envision the same society—one that has no need for punitive institutions like prisons, police and foster care to ensure community well-being and safety. Without attention to the foster industrial complex, however, reform proposals might help to strengthen it—thereby expanding the carceral state rather than shrinking it.

A more expansive understanding of abolition is essential to collectively building a new society that supports rather than destroys families and communities.

Dorothy Roberts, *Abolishing Policing Also Means Abolishing Family Regulation*, THE IMPRINT (Jun. 16, 2020, 5:26 AM), https://imprint news.org/child-welfare-2/abolishing-policing-also-means-abolishing-family-regulation/44480. See also DOROTHY ROBERTS, TORN APART: HOW THE CHILD WELFARE SYSTEM DESTROYS BLACK FAMILIES—AND HOW ABOLITION CAN BUILD A SAFER WORLD (2022). Other scholars have made similar calls for abolition of the child welfare system. *See, e.g.,* Cynthia Godsoe, *An Abolitionist Horizon for Child Welfare*, L. & POL. ECON. PROJECT (Aug. 6, 2020), https://lpeproject.org/blog/an-abolitionist-horizon-for-child-welfare/ ("Like the criminal system, the family policing and regulation system needs an abolitionist horizon and any reforms that increase its funding or net-widening should be opposed. Instead, power should be given to communities who are best positioned to keep their children safe, and the state should give families the support they need, such as cash grants, affordable housing, child care, and food, without the specter of child removal as the backdrop."); Alan J. Dettlaff et al., *It is not a Broken System, it is a System that Needs to be Broken: The upEND Movement to Abolish the Child Welfare System*, 14 J. PUB. CHILD WELFARE 500 (2020) (arguing that "[t]he child welfare system disproportionately harms Black children and families through systemic over-surveillance, over-involvement, and the resulting adverse outcomes associated with foster care. Ending this harm will only be achieved when the forcible surveillance and separation of children from their parents is no longer viewed as an acceptable form of intervention."). How would you respond to these arguments? What do you make of their grounding in the authority of communities regulated by family law rules? How should these voices and views by accommodated by those who are setting family law rules?

What would abolition of the child welfare system look like? Some scholars have explained that:

> Abolition of child welfare does not mean abandoning the need to protect children. It means building new ways of protecting and supporting families that also dismantle coercive systems of surveillance and punishment. It means engaging in the work of building radically different systems of care that recognize the basic need of children to be with their families in safe and supportive communities. . . .
>
>   . . .
>
> The road to abolition is not intended to dismantle the child welfare system and leave nothing in its place. . . .
>
> The road to abolition means giving families and communities access to mental health services, to jobs that pay living wages, to well-funded public schools, to health care, to homes—especially homes free from environmental toxins—to child care, and to community-based interventions to stop harm from occurring in the first place. When harm does occur, mechanisms of support should be designed to not cause more harm by separating families, punishing parents and fragmenting communities. Rather, they should support families in figuring out what is needed for healing, safety, and the prevention of future harm.

Alan J. Dettlaff et al., *What it Means to Abolish Child Welfare as We Know It*, THE IMPRINT (Oct. 14, 2020), https://imprintnews.org/race/what-means-abolish-child-welfare/48257. For further discussion, *see. e.g.*, Chris Gottlieb, *Black Families Are Outraged About Family Separation Within the U.S. It's Time to Listen to Them*, TIME (Mar. 17, 2021), https://time.com/5946929/child-welfare-black-families/; Symposium, *Strengthened Bonds: Abolishing the Child Welfare System and Re-Envisioning Child Well*-Being, 11 COLUM. J. RACE & L. 1 (2021), https://journals.library.columbia.edu/index.php/cjrl/announcement/view/414.

Professor Anna Arons argues that the COVID-19 pandemic created an unexpected opportunity to experience a "short-term experiment in abolition." Anna Arons, *An Unintended Abolition: Family Regulation During the COVID-19 Crisis*, 12 COLUM. J. RACE & L. 1 (2022). She writes:

> Abolition of the family regulation system is too often dismissed as a fantasy, an impracticable ideal that cannot be tested in reality. Yet the COVID-19 crisis provided exactly such a test: for several months, in much of the country, the family regulation system ceased to function as usual and instead was reduced to its bare bones. New York City, the initial epicenter of the crisis, shut down in mid-March 2020 and remained under near-total lock-down until mid-June. During that time, mandated reporters and agency caseworkers were sidelined and courts limited their operations. Reports of child neglect and abuse fell, the number of cases filed in family court fell, and the number of families separated by the government fell. Meanwhile, in the absence of government

assistance—and government intrusion—communities developed robust mutual aid projects to meet their needs for food, provisions, childcare, and therapeutic services.

As the first wave of the COVID-19 crisis receded in New York City, family regulation system operations began to normalize. But while the predominant media narrative predicted that the pandemic and accompanying social isolation would increase child neglect and abuse, the numbers did not bear that out: during New York's shutdown, child fatalities fell, as did reports of child neglect and child abuse. This trend continued into the fall: there was no surge in reports even once mandated reporters began to re-enter the field. With fewer government-sanctioned separations of families, children stayed just as safe.

. . .

Though unintentional, this brief experiment shows that the typical outsized and reactionary family regulation system is not necessary to protect children; indeed, most children who are separated from their families are safer at home. Instead, the problems that the system typically purports to address—namely child poverty—can be addressed in a radically reduced and re-envisioned system that relies on principles of mutual aid rather than government-led oppression. Abolition need not be a fantasy; New York City already made it, for a moment, a reality.

Id. at 2, 4–5. Is "this brief experiment" enough for you to imagine larger-scale experiments in abolition? As you read the materials below, consider how caseworkers and agency officials responding to alleged child maltreatment might respond to arguments for abolition.

For discussion of the harms to children of removal from their home and placement in foster care, *see* Shanta Trivedi, *The Harm of Child Removal*, 43 N.Y.U. REV. L. & SOC. CHANGE 523 (2019).

a.   DEFINING NEGLECT

On page 386 of the Unabridged 7th edition, and on page 287 of the Concise 7th edition, replace notes 1 and 2 with the following:

1.   How should the Office of Administrative Law resolve this case on remand? The Division of Child Protection and Permanency ("the Division") proceedings are confidential so the outcome on remand is not public. *See* Email from Sean Marotta, attorney for E.D.-O. to Jessica Peslak, Research Assistant for Prof. Solangel Maldonado, Seton Hall University School of Law (Feb. 7, 2019, 4:34 EST) (on file with author) (explaining why he could not "share the ultimate outcome on remand").

The caseworker's investigation of the home did not reveal any risk to the children. Indeed, the caseworker concluded that the children appeared to be well-nurtured. Furthermore, there was no evidence that the children had been left unattended before or that E.D.-O. would leave them unattended again. Given these facts, why did the Division file a complaint in

Superior Court against E.D.-O. and her husband seeking care and supervision of their four children? Why did the deputy attorney general oppose E.D.-O's motion for an administrative hearing to appeal the substantiation of neglect finding? Why did the Director of the Division grant the state's motion and deny E.D.-O's request for a hearing? According to Ms. Erin O'Leary, who represented the Division in *E.D.-O*, the State opposed E.D.-O's motion for an administrative hearing because there were no disputed facts—E.D.-O. left a young child unattended in the vehicle. Conversation with Erin O'Leary, Assistant Att'y Gen., Dep't of Child. and Families Practice Group—State of New Jersey (Jun. 16, 2021). The lack of any material facts in dispute was the legal basis for the State's motion for a summary finding. *Id.*

E.D.-O's daughter did not suffer any harm as a result of E.D.-O's conduct. Is it relevant that, as Ms. O'Leary explains, "the Division—and other child welfare agencies around the country—are often confronted with cases where children who are left unattended in vehicles suffer serious harm and even death"? *Id.*

2.   Parents who leave a child unattended in a vehicle not uncommonly face civil and criminal penalties, including loss of custody, probation, community service, incarceration, and placement in the state's child abuse registry. *See* George L. Blum, *Criminal Prosecutions and Civil Actions for Leaving Child in Unattended Hot or Cold Vehicle*, 26 A.L.R.7th Art. 5 (2017). E.D.-O. argued that it was unreasonable to place her on the state's child abuse registry given the circumstances of this case. Should an agency have discretion to determine whether the circumstances of a particular case warrant an exception to placement in the registry?

The consequences of having one's name included in the registry are substantial. In addition to the potential reputational harms, it may impede a person's ability to obtain employment and certainly any employment involving contact with children. It may also disqualify a person from becoming a foster or adoptive parent. *See Kane v. Comm'r of Dep't of Health & Human Servs.*, 960 A.2d 1196, 1202 (Me. 2008) (holding that "[t]he stigma of being listed as 'substantiated' for child abuse combined with the adverse professional and social consequences of being listed in the database implicates a fundamental liberty interest.").

On page 398 of the Unabridged 7th edition, replace the Note with the following:

1.   Why might the defendant not have sought medical attention for her stepdaughter Shanaya? The perpetrator of the abuse, the child's father in this case, is criminally liable. Are there public policy reasons for also prosecuting a parent or guardian who fails to protect a child from abuse perpetrated by another parent? Commentators have argued that failure to protect laws disproportionately punish mothers who are often victims of domestic violence. *See, e.g.*, Jeanne A. Fugate, *Who's Failing Whom? A Critical Look at Failure-to-Protect Laws*, 76 N.Y.U. L. REV. 272 (2001).

2.   When a parent fails to protect a child from physical or sexual abuse by another person, including abuse by another parent, the state may intervene and remove the child from the care of the parent who failed to protect the child. A parent's failure to protect a child from abuse may constitute neglect. *See, e.g.,* COLO. REV. STAT. ANN. § 19–3–102(1) (West 2022) ("A child is neglected . . . if . . . a parent, guardian, or legal custodian has . . . allowed another to mistreat or abuse the child without taking lawful means to stop such mistreatment or abuse and prevent it from recurring"); D.C. CODE ANN. § 16–2301(9)(A) (West 2022) ("The term 'neglected child' means a child . . . whose parent, guardian, or custodian has failed to make reasonable efforts to prevent the infliction of abuse upon the child."); *see also* RESTATEMENT OF THE LAW, CHILDREN AND THE LAW § 2.24(b)(3) (AM. L. INST., Tentative Draft No. 2, 2019) (defining physical neglect to include the "failure to protect a child from physical abuse by another person if the parent, guardian, or custodian knew or reasonably should have known of the harm or risk of harm to the child and failed to take reasonable precautionary measures to protect the child from harm"); *New Jersey Div. of Child Prot. & Permanency v. K.N.S.,* 119 A.3d 235, 239 (N.J. App. Div. 2015) (affirming adjudication of neglect against a mother who failed to protect her 7 month-old son who was physically abused by the mother's boyfriend when she left the child in his care knowing that that he was "untrustworthy and impatient"); *In re Michael I,* 276 A.D.2d 839 (N.Y. App. Div. 2000) (affirming adjudication of neglect against the mother who knew or should have known that the father was abusing the child but failed to prevent abuse by the father).

b.   RELIGIOUS PRACTICE OR NEGLECT?

On page 404 of the Unabridged 7th edition, and on page 297 of the Concise 7th edition, replace note 3 with the following:

3.   Although every state requires proof that a child has received the statutorily required immunizations before enrolling in school, the majority of states have statutes recognizing religious exemptions to vaccination. Approximately one-third of states also allow philosophical (personal belief) exemptions. A number of states, including California, Connecticut, Maine, and New York, have repealed their religious exemptions to vaccination in recent years. Claims that the repeal of religious exemptions violates the First Amendment's guarantee of free exercise of religion have been unsuccessful, *see F.F. v. State,* 194 A.D.3d 80 (N.Y. App. Div. 3d Dept 2021), and the U.S. Supreme Court has long held that a parent "cannot claim freedom from compulsory vaccination for a child . . . on religious grounds." *Prince v. Massachusetts,* 321 U.S. 158, 166–67 (1944) (holding that "[t]he right to practice religion freely does not include liberty to expose the community or the child to communicable disease . . ."). Given the Supreme Court's decision in *Fulton,* Chapter 1, *supra,* and other rulings for religious worshippers in the COVID-19 era, *see, e.g., Tandon v. Newsom,* 141 S.Ct. 1294 (2021) (granting injunctive relief to plaintiffs asserting that California's restrictions on private gatherings during COVID-19 pandemic violated their rights to, *inter alia,* free exercise under the First Amendment), will states now be under pressure to reconsider the operations of their religious exemptions? Does it seem likely to you that the Supreme Court will reaffirm its prior

position that the Free Exercise Clause does not require that the state provide exemptions from vaccination?

Parents have deeply held religious and philosophical objections to vaccination. How should the law balance parental authority with children's best interests and public health? For an article discussing parents' reasons for not vaccinating their children and the resulting risks to public health, *see* Dorit Rubinstein Reiss & Lois A. Weithorn, *Responding to the Childhood Vaccination Crisis: Legal Frameworks and Tools in the Context of Parental Vaccine Refusal*, 63 BUFF. L. REV. 881 (2015).

4.   The majority of states require parental consent before a minor may be vaccinated. The COVID-19 pandemic highlighted the tension between parental authority to make medical decisions about a child's health care, the child's interests in their health, and the states' interest in protecting its citizens and public health from communicable diseases. What should states do when an adolescent seeks to be vaccinated against COVID-19 but the parent refuses consent? *See* Jan Hoffman, A*s Parents Forbid Covid Shots, Defiant Teenagers Seek Ways to Get Them*, N.Y. TIMES (June 26, 2021), https://www.nytimes.com/2021/06/26/health/covid-vaccine-teens-consent. html; Tara Haelle, *Can Teens Get Vaccinated If Their Parents Object?*, NATIONAL GEOGRAPHIC (May 25, 2021), https://www.nationalgeographic. com/science/article/can-teens-get-vaccinated-if-their-parents-object; Sharon Terlep, *Covid-19 Shots for Teens Can Hit Legal Snags and Parental Pushback*, WALL ST. J. (May 19, 2021), https://www.wsj.com/articles/covid-19-shots-for-teens-can-hit-legal-snags-and-parental-pushback-116214166 03. A minority of states allow adolescents above a certain age to consent to the human papillomavirus vaccine ("HPV") which prevents certain cancers caused by sexually transmitted diseases. Should states enact laws allowing minors to consent to the COVID-19 vaccine? *See* Larissa Morgan et al., *COVID-19 Vaccination of Minors Without Parental Consent: Respecting Emerging Autonomy and Advancing Public Health*. 175 JAMA PEDIATR. 995 (2021) (recommending that minors 12 years of age and older be allowed to consent to the COVID-19 vaccine without parental approval but recommending that minors under the age of 15 receive "support and facilitation from their clinicians and other trusted adult figures" when making the decision).

D. ADOPTION

3. STANDARDS

c.   ADOPTION OF NATIVE AMERICAN CHILDREN

On page 530 of the Unabridged 7th edition, and on page 407 of the Concise 7th edition, replace note 3 with the following:

3.   How much is the majority's holding driven by equal protection concerns along the lines of race? Native-Americans hold a unique legal status in the United States stemming from tribes' position as independent, sovereign nations before European settlers came to the United States. *See* Maggie

Blackhawk, *Federal Indian Law as Paradigm Within Public Law*, 132 HARV. L. REV. 1787, 1796 (2019) (noting that the United States "recognize[s] the inherent sovereignty of Native Nations within its borders"). Earlier decisions by the Supreme Court have "squarely" held "that classifications based on Indian tribal membership are not impermissible racial classifications." *Adoptive Couple v. Baby Girl*, 570 U.S. 637, 690 (2013) (Sotomayor, J., dissenting); *Morton v. Mancari*, 417 U.S. 535, 554 (1974) (recognizing that federal law does not treat Native Americans as "a discrete racial group, but, rather as members of quasi-sovereign tribal entities"). Does the majority's "references to the fact that Baby Girl is 3/256 Cherokee by ancestry," *Adoptive Couple*, 570 U.S. at 690 (Sotomayor, J., dissenting), raise the specter that the ICWA—if not interpreted as the majority opinion interprets it—may be tantamount to a constitutionally illegitimate "one drop" or, more exactly, a "3/256's drop" rule?

In 2017, seven individuals who wished to adopt or foster "Indian children" (as defined under ICWA), a birth mother who wished to place her Indian child for adoption with a non-Indian family, and the States of Texas, Louisiana, and Indiana challenged the constitutionality of the ICWA in federal court in Texas. The district court ruled that the ICWA's placement preferences violate the Fifth Amendment's guarantee of equal protection because they are based on race. *Brackeen v. Zinke*, 338 F.Supp.3d 514, 536 (N.D. Tex. 2018). The district court held that the ICWA is a "race-based statute" and is not narrowly tailored to Congress's obligations to Indian tribes because it grants preference to any Native American family over a non-Native family even if the Native American family belongs to a different tribe than the child. *Id.* at 534.

A three-judge panel of the U.S. Court of Appeals for the Fifth Circuit reversed and held that the ICWA's definition of an Indian child was not a race-based classification for constitutional equal protection purposes. *Brackeen v. Bernhardt*, 937 F.3d 406, 426 (5th Cir. 2019). Plaintiffs petitioned for rehearing *en banc* and an *en banc* majority agreed with the three-judge panel's holding "that ICWA's 'Indian child' classification does not violate equal protection." *Brackeen v. Haaland*, 994 F.3d 249, 267–68 (5th Cir. 2019) (*en banc*) (*per curiam*). The *en banc* court, however, split evenly on the equal protection challenge to ICWA's adoptive placement preference for "other Indian families," and its foster care placement preference for a licensed "Indian foster home." The result of this even split on this question was to affirm without a precedential opinion the district court's ruling that the preference for "other Indian families," and for a licensed "Indian foster home" violate equal protection. *Id.* at 268.

Writing for the *en banc* majority that held "that ICWA's 'Indian child' classification does not violate equal protection," *id.* at 267–68 & n.3, Circuit Judge James L. Dennis explained:

> . . . [W]e cannot say that simply because ICWA's definition of "Indian child" includes minors eligible for tribal membership (who have a biological parent who is a tribal member), the classification is drawn along racial lines. Tribal eligibility does not inherently turn on race, but rather on the criteria set by the tribes, which are

present-day political entities.[50] Just as the United States or any other sovereign may choose to whom it extends citizenship, so too may the Indian tribes. . . . That tribes may use ancestry as part of their criteria for determining membership eligibility does not change that ICWA does not classify in this way; instead, ICWA's Indian child designation classifies on the basis of a child's connection to a political entity based on whatever criteria that political entity may prescribe. [*See Santa Clara Pueblo v. Martinez,* 436 U.S. 49, 72 n.32 (1978)] ("A tribe's right to define its own membership for tribal purposes has long been recognized as central to its existence as an independent political community.") . . .

Id. at 337–38 (Dennis, Circuit Judge).

Judge Dennis and Judge Duncan each wrote separate opinions addressing the issues that did not garner an *en banc* majority, including the question on which the *en banc* court equally divided—whether "ICWA's adoptive placement preference for 'other Indian families' . . . and its foster care placement preference for a licensed 'Indian foster home . . . .' " violate equal protection. *Id.* at 268. Concluding that ICWA's placement preferences do not violate equal protection, Judge Dennis wrote:

> Plaintiffs also separately contend that ICWA's lowest-tiered adoptive placement preference for "other Indian families" constitutes a racial classification. . . . This preference, they argue, treats Indian tribes as "fungible" and does not account for the array of differences between tribes, which, in turn, evinces a desire to keep Indian children within a larger Indian "race." We disagree. . . . [T]his adoption placement preference—like all of ICWA's placement preferences—"applies only to members of federally recognized tribes." [*Morton v. Mancari,* 417 U.S. 535, 554 n.24 (1974)]; see also 25 U.S.C. § 1903(3) (defining "Indian" as encompassing only members of federally recognized tribes). Because on its face the provision is limited to "members of federally recognized tribes," "the preference is political rather than racial in

---

[50] As the Tribes explain, under some tribal membership laws, eligibility extends to children without Indian blood, such as the descendants of persons formerly enslaved by tribes who became members after they were freed or the descendants of persons of any ethnicity who have been adopted into a tribe. *See, e.g.,* Treaty with the Cherokees, 1866, U.S.—Cherokee Nation of Indians, art. 9, July 19, 1866, 14 Stat. 799 (providing that the Cherokee Nation "further agree that all freedmen who have been liberated by voluntary act of their former owners or by law, as well as all free colored persons who were in the country at the commencement of the rebellion, and are now residents therein, or who may return within six months, and their descendants, shall have all the rights of native Cherokees"); *Cherokee Nation v. Nash,* 267 F.Supp.3d 86, 132, 140–41 (D.D.C. 2017) (holding that Cherokee Freedmen enjoy full citizenship rights as members of the Cherokee Nation because Congress has never abrogated or amended the relevant treaty terms). Accordingly, a child may fall under ICWA's membership eligibility standard because his or her biological parent became a member of a tribe, despite not being racially Indian. Additionally, many racially Indian children, such as those affiliated with non-federally recognized tribes, do not fall within ICWA's definition of "Indian child." When it comes to ICWA's definition of Indian child, race is thus both underinclusive—because it does not capture these descendants of freed enslaved persons or other adoptive members who are not "racially" Indians—and overinclusive—because it embraces "racially" Indian children who are not enrolled in or eligible for membership in a recognized tribe or who lack a biological parent who is a member of a recognized tribe.

nature." *Mancari*, 417 U.S. at 554 n.24. Accordingly, it, too, is subject only to rational basis review.

　. . .

　. . . [Congress] enacted ICWA "to protect the best interests of Indian children and to promote the stability and security of Indian tribes and families." [25 U.S.C. § 1902]. By systematically favoring the placement of Indian children with Indian tribes and families in child custody proceedings, Congress sought to ensure that children who are eligible for tribal membership are raised in environments that engender respect for the traditions and values of Indian tribes, thereby increasing the likelihood that the child will eventually join a tribe and contribute to "the continued existence and integrity of Indian tribes." *Id.* § 1901(3). . . .

Id. at 340–41 (Dennis, Circuit Judge).

In response to the claim that "ICWA uses *impermissible means* to further Congress's obligations to the Indian tribes, *id.* at 341, Judge Dennis explained that:

　. . . It is rational to think that ensuring that an Indian child is raised in a household that respects Indian values and traditions makes it more likely that the child will eventually join an Indian tribe—thus "promot[ing] the stability and security of Indian tribes," 25 U.S.C. § 1902—even when the child's parents would rather the child be placed with a non-Indian family. And we reject the notion that ICWA's preference for Indian families treats tribes as fungible. As Defendants point out, many contemporary tribes descended from larger historical bands and continue to share close relationships and linguistic, cultural, and religious traditions, so placing a child with another Indian family could conceivably further the interest in maintaining the child's ties with his or her tribe or culture. . . . By providing a preference for placing Indian children with a family that is part of a formally recognized Indian political community that is interconnected to the child's own tribe, ICWA enables that child to avail herself of the numerous benefits— both tangible and intangible—that come from being raised within this context. And even if this were not the case, Congress could rationally conclude that placing an Indian child with a different tribe would fortify the ranks of that other tribe, contributing to the continued existence of the Indian tribes as a whole. . . .

　In sum, § 1903(4)'s definition of an "Indian child" and § 1915(a)(3)'s Indian family preference can be rationally linked to the trust relationship between the tribes and the federal government, as well as to furthering tribal sovereignty and self-government. They therefore do not violate constitutional equal protection principles, and the district court erred by concluding otherwise. . . .

Id. at 345 (Dennis, Circuit Judge).

In a separate opinion joined by the judges who concluded that ICWA's preferences for "other Indian families," and for a licensed "Indian foster home" violate equal protection, Judge Stuart Kyle Duncan wrote:

> We agree with Plaintiffs that a naked preference for Indian over non-Indian families does nothing to further ICWA's stated aim of ensuring that Indian children are linked to their tribe. This conclusion follows *a fortiori* from our conclusion that ICWA's Indian child category is insufficiently linked to federal tribal interests. The Indian child category encompassed children who were not, and may never be, members of a tribe. Even more, ICWA's preference for "Indian families" lacks any connection to a child's tribe: as explained, the Indian families preferred over non-Indian families are, by definition, not members of the child's tribe. Thus, the preference has no rational link to maintaining a child's links with his tribe. . . .
>
> . . . Defendants argue that this "Indian family" preference is not merely a "preference for 'generic "Indianness." ' " They assert it instead "reflects the reality that many tribes have deep historic and cultural connections with other tribes, and that many Indian children may be eligible for membership in more than one tribe." We are unpersuaded. Even accepting that some tribes are interrelated, ICWA's Indian family preference is not limited in that way. Rather, the preference privileges Indian families of *any* tribe, regardless of their connection to the child's tribe, over all non-Indian families. ICWA's classification therefore does not rationally further linking children to their tribes.
>
> In sum, we conclude ICWA's preferring Indian over non-Indian families violates the equal protection component of the Fifth Amendment.

Id. at 401 (Duncan, Circuit Judge).

As noted, the States of Texas, Louisiana, and Indiana joined the individual plaintiffs challenging the constitutionality of the ICWA in *Brackeen.* Judge Dennis observed that:

> Combined [the State plaintiffs—], Texas, Louisiana, Indiana, and Ohio (which filed an amicus brief in support of Plaintiffs) are home to only about 1% of the total number of federally recognized Indian tribes and less than 4% of the national American Indian and Alaska Native population. On the other hand, twenty-six other states and the District of Columbia have filed amicus briefs asking us to uphold ICWA and the Final Rule. Those states are California, Alaska, Arizona, Colorado, Connecticut, Idaho, Illinois, Iowa, Maine, Massachusetts, Michigan, Minnesota, Mississippi, Montana, Nevada, New Jersey, New Mexico, New York, Oklahoma, Oregon, Pennsylvania, Rhode Island, Utah, Virginia, Washington, and Wisconsin, which are collectively home to 94% of federally recognized Indian tribes and 69% of the national American Indian and Alaska Native population.

We do not decide cases by a show of hands of states' votes, of course, but we cannot ignore the irony of the situation with which we are faced. Twenty-six states and the District of Columbia, which are home to a large majority of federally recognized tribes and the nation's overall indigenous population, do not view ICWA as any sort of burden on their child welfare systems. They strongly contend that ICWA is constitutional and have no problem applying it in their state court systems; indeed, they view ICWA as the "gold standard" for child welfare practices and a "critical tool" in managing their relationships with the Indian tribes within their borders. Conversely, only four states with relatively few tribes and Indians regard ICWA as offensive to their sovereignty and seek to have the law struck down completely because it intrudes upon their otherwise unimpeded discretion to manage child custody proceedings involving Indian children . . .

Brackeen, 994 F.3d at 270 (Dennis, Circuit Judge). What is the significance, if any, of the overwhelming support of the ICWA by the states where the majority of the Indian population resides?

In February 2022 the Supreme Court agreed to hear *Brackeen v. Haaland* and will address, among other questions, whether ICWA's placement preferences discriminate on the basis of race in violation of the U.S. Constitution. See *Brackeen v. Haaland*, 142 S.Ct. 1205 (2022).

d.   SEXUAL ORIENTATION

On page 537 of the Unabridged 7th edition, replace the note with the following text:

Even after the Supreme Court's decision in *Obergefell*, some faith-based adoption agencies refuse to place children with gay or lesbian couples. A number of states expressly allow agencies to refuse services on grounds of religious conscience. *See* MICH. COMP. LAWS ANN. § 400.5a (West 2022) (prohibiting the state from taking "an adverse action against a child placing agency on the basis that the child placing agency has declined or will decline to provide services that conflict with, or provide services under circumstances that conflict with, the child placing agency's sincerely held religious beliefs contained in a written policy, statement of faith, or other document adhered to by the child placing agency."); *see also* ALA. CODE § 26–10D–5 (West 2022); S.D. CODIFIED LAWS § 26–6–41 (West 2022); TEX. HUM. RES. CODE ANN. § 45.005 (West 2021). For information about each state's policies on adoption and foster care by LGBTQIA+ families, see *Foster and Adoption Laws*, MOVEMENT ADVANCEMENT PROJECT, https://www.lgbtmap. org/equality-maps/foster_and_adoption_laws.

Fulton v. City of Philadelphia

Supreme Court of the United States, 2021.
593 U.S. ___, 141 S.Ct. 1868, 210 L.Ed.2d 137.

Reproduced in Chapter 1 *supra*, p. 1.

CHAPTER 6

ASSISTED REPRODUCTIVE TECHNOLOGIES AND THE LAW

D. DISPOSITION OF GAMETES AND EMBRYOS

On page 746 of the Unabridged 7th edition, and on page 544 of the Concise 7th edition, replace note 4 with the following notes, then renumber the remaining notes:

4. Actress Sofia Vergara has been embroiled in a long battle with her former fiancé, Nicholas Loeb, regarding the fate of the two pre-embryos they created and cryopreserved while they were still a couple and planning on having children via IVF and gestational surrogacy. The pre-embryos were created in the fall of 2013. The couple broke their engagement in May of 2014. Loeb notified Vergara that he wanted to transfer the pre-embryos to a surrogate and she objected. He initially filed suit in a California court, but eventually withdrew the lawsuit. He then named the frozen pre-embryos Emma and Isabella and created a trust to benefit the pre-embryos, suing Vergara in their name, this time in a Louisiana court. Loeb claimed that both parties to the dispute had a connection to the state, but it seems that the legal framework analyzed in the previous note could have played a central role in the choice of jurisdiction. Vergara removed the case to federal court in New Orleans and won the case, on the basis of lack of subject matter jurisdiction. Following the dismissal, Loeb became a resident of Louisiana and sued again. Vergara tried to remove the case to federal court again, but this time, Loeb invoked the state's Uniform Child Custody and Jurisdiction Act, and the federal court dismissed Vergara's motion, agreeing with Loeb that this was a custody case, and a federal court therefore did not have jurisdiction. *See* Drew Broach, *Sofia Vergara Embryo Lawsuit Moves to Plaquemines Parish Court*, NOLA (June 27, 2018) https://www.nola. com/crime/index.ssf/2018/06/sofia_vergara_embryo_lawsuit.html; *Human Embryo #4 HB-A By & Through Emma & Isabella Louisiana Tr. No. 1 v. Vergara*, No. CV 17–1498, 2017 WL 3686569, at *1 (E.D. La. Aug. 25, 2017). On the questions of jurisdiction raised in this case see *infra*, Chapter 10.

The Louisiana part of the dispute ended in January 2021, when the Fourth Circuit Court of Appeal in Louisiana ruled that Loeb was not a resident of Louisiana but had instead engaged in forum shopping. The court also analyzed whether cryopreserved pre-embryos or unborn embryos qualified as "children" under the Uniform Child Custody and Jurisdiction Act, and concluded that they didn't. *See Loeb v. Vergara*, 313 So.3d 346 (2021). What would have been the potential consequences of legally treating pre-embryos as similar to actual children for other areas of reproductive rights? What would be the consequences of such treatment for the constitutionally protected right to an abortion, for example? In March 2021, Vergara was granted a permanent injunction against Loeb in a California court, which prevents him from using any of the pre-embryos without her written consent. *See* Order Granting Plaintiff's Motion for Summary Adjudication and Permanent Injunction, *Vergara v. Loeb*, No. BC 650580 (Cal. Super. Ct., L.A. Cnty., Mar. 2, 2021). For a revealing analysis of how courts treat male consent to reproduction see Dara E. Purvis, *Frozen Embryos, Male Consent, and Masculinities*, 97 IND. L. J. 611 (2021) .

5. In *Dobbs v. Jackson Women's Health Org.*, 597 U.S. ___, 142 S.Ct. 2228 (2022), the Supreme Court overturned the right to an abortion. Medical professionals and academics working in the field of ART are concerned about *Dobbs'* potential effects on IVF. One of the most urgent questions seems to be whether the abortion bans that will take effect in a number of jurisdictions will apply to frozen embryos, making it hard for patients to make independent decisions about frozen embryo disposition and increasing the legal risks for medical professionals involved in the process of creating them. Some academics have observed that Justice Alito's insistence that abortion is different than other rights because it destroys "potential life," might leave the creation or destruction of embryos in the IVF process "on the wrong side of constitutional protection." *See* I. Glenn Cohen et al., *What Overturning Roe v Wade May Mean for Assisted Reproductive Technologies in the US*, 328 JAMA 15 (2022). From a medical care perspective, IVF patients and professionals are concerned about the limitations potentially imposed on access to healthcare in cases of miscarriage and ectopic pregnancies, among other scenarios. *See* Lisa H. Harris, *Navigating Loss of Abortion Services— A Large Academic Medical Center Prepares for the Overturn of Roe v. Wade*, 386 N. Engl. J. Med. 2061, 2063 (2022). Some commentators observe that *Dobbs'* effects largely depend on political will, which means that *Dobbs* may or may not impact IVF depending on the current projects and political power of pro-life constituencies in different states and in Congress. *See* Cohen et al., *supra*, at 16.

CHAPTER 8

CUSTODY

C. APPLYING THE BEST INTERESTS STANDARD

3. RACE AND ETHNICITY

On page 959 of the Unabridged 7th edition, and on page 626 of the Concise 7th edition, replace note 2 with the following:

2. What is the role of race in custody disputes after *Palmore*? In *In re Marriage of Gambla*, the Illinois Court of Appeals affirmed a trial court's custody award of an African-American and Caucasian child to her African-American mother over her Caucasian father, concluding that the child "would have to learn to exist as a biracial woman in a society that is sometimes hostile to such individuals and [the African-American mother] would be better able to provide for [the child's] emotional needs in this respect. 853 N.E.2d 847, 868 (Ill. App. Ct. 2006), *abrogated by People v. McKown*, 924 N.E.2d 941 (Ill. 2010). In distinguishing *Marriage of Gambla* from *Palmore*, the court explained that "the custody award [in *Palmore*] was unconstitutional, not because the trial court considered race, but because the trial court considered *solely* race" and added that "[v]olumes of cases from other jurisdictions have interpreted *Palmore* as not prohibiting the consideration of race in matters of child custody." *Id.* at 869 (citing cases).

In *Christie BB. v. Isaiah CC.*, 194 A.D.3d 1130 (N.Y. App. Div. 3d Dept 2021), an appellate court ordered a mother to remove a "small confederate flag painted on a rock near her driveway" or risk losing custody of her mixed-race daughter. *Id.* at 1134. The parents had stipulated to joint legal and physical custody of their daughter when she was three years old. *Id.* at 1130. A year later, the mother filed a petition for modification seeking primary physical custody and the father filed a counter-petition seeking sole custody. *Id.* After a fact-finding hearing, the trial court continued the joint legal and physical custody order but amended its prior order to provide that the mother's home would be the child's primary residence for the purpose of schooling. *Id.* at 1131. On appeal, the Appellate Division explained:

> [A]lthough not addressed by Family Court or the attorney for the child, the mother's testimony at the hearing, as well as an exhibit admitted into evidence, reveal that she has a small confederate flag painted on a rock near her driveway. Given that the child is of mixed race, it would seem apparent that the presence of the flag is not in the child's best interests, as the mother must encourage and teach the child to embrace her mixed race identity, rather than thrust her into a world that only makes sense through the tortured lens of cognitive dissonance. Further, and viewed pragmatically, the presence of the confederate flag is a symbol inflaming the already strained relationship between the parties. As such, while recognizing that the First Amendment protects the mother's right

to display the flag ... if it is not removed by June 1, 2021, its continued presence shall constitute a change in circumstances and Family Court shall factor this into any future best interests analysis.

Id. at 1134. What do you think of the court's order? Would it survive constitutional muster? Is the court making assumptions about the mother's embrace or rejection of her daughter's racial background based on the presence of a confederate flag near her driveway? If so, should it? Does the mother's testimony that "she has never used any racial slurs in front of the child or at all" change your view of this case? Given a parent's fundamental right to make decisions about their child's upbringing, *see Troxel v. Granville,* 530 U.S. 57, 66 (2000), can a court require a parent to "encourage and teach the child to embrace her mixed-race identity," as this court does? What if a parent determines that it is in the mixed-race child's best interest to raise them as White? How might that be different from a parent who decides to raise a mixed-race child as Black? The father in this case believes that the mother is not helping the child to understand her heritage and that the mother is teaching the child that she is White. Email from Andrea J. Mooney, Clinical Prof. of Law (ret.), Cornell Law School, to Jonathan Ross, Research Assistant for Prof. Solangel Maldonado, Seton Hall University School of Law (July 1, 2021 11:02 EDT) (on file with author).

For discussion of post-*Palmore* cases considering race as a factor in a custody dispute, *see* Solangel Maldonado, *Bias in the Family: Race, Ethnicity, and Culture in Custody Disputes,* 55 FAM. CT. REV. 213 (2017). For a comprehensive analysis of the role of race in custody disputes, adoption, and foster care, *see* Katie Eyer, *Constitutional Colorblindness and the Family,* 162 U. PA. L. REV. 537 (2014).

5.   RELIGION

On page 973 of the Unabridged 7th edition, and on page 640 of the Concise 7th edition, replace note 2 with the following:

2.   In *Cohen v. Cohen,* 182 A.D.3d 545 (N.Y. App. Div. 2d Dept 2020), the same court that decided *Weisberger* held that a trial court's order directing a non-custodial father "to comply with the 'cultural norms' of Hasidic Judaism during his periods of parental access" was unconstitutional. *Id.* at 546. When the parties divorced, the court awarded the mother sole legal custody of the two minor children and granted the father parental access. *Id.* at 545. "Recognizing that the children had been raised during the marriage in accordance with the practices and beliefs of Satmar Hasidic Judaism, the [trial court] directed the father to provide the children with exclusively kosher food and to make 'all reasonable efforts to ensure that the children's appearance and conduct comply with the 'Hasidic' religious requirements of the [mother] and of the children's schools as they were raised while the children are in [his] physical custody.'" *Id.* at 545. A few months later, the mother moved to modify the judgment and complained that "the father had failed to himself comply with Hasidic religious requirements in the presence of the children during his periods of parental access." *Id.* at 546. Although it was undisputed "that the father did not prevent the children from practicing their religion during his periods of parental access," the trial court ordered him to "conduct himself in accordance with the cultural norms" of Hasidic Judaism established by the parents during the marriage." *Id.* On appeal the Appellate Division held that the trial court's order "ran afoul of constitutional limitations by compelling the father to himself practice a religion, rather than merely directing him to provide the children with a religious upbringing." *Id.* at 546–47. Is *Cohen* distinguishable from *Weisberger*?

3.   The challenges presented when parents have diverse religious views or practices may also exist when one parent is a non-believer. In *Elk Grove Unified Sch. Dist. v. Newdow*, 542 U.S. 1 (2004), *abrogated by Lexmark Int'l, Inc. v. Static Control Components, Inc.*, 572 U.S. 118 (2014), a father who was an atheist challenged a school district's policy of leading students, including his kindergarten-age daughter, in the daily recitation of the Pledge of Allegiance because it contains the words "under God." He argued that the district's policy constitutes religious indoctrination in violation of the First Amendment's Free Exercise and Establishment Clauses. *Id.* at 5. The child's mother, who was a Christian and had the authority under a duly entered custody order to make final decisions about the child's welfare if the parents disagreed, sought leave to intervene and dismiss the suit. *Id.* at 9. Noting that the state court had deprived the father of the right to sue on his daughter's behalf, the Supreme Court held that the father lacked standing to invoke the jurisdiction of the federal courts to shield his daughter from religious views that the mother endorsed. *Id.* at 17–18.

G. MODIFICATION

1. CHANGE IN CIRCUMSTANCES

On page 1052 of the Unabridged 7th edition, and on page 715 of the Concise 7th edition, replace notes 2 and 3 with the following:

2.   The *Smith* court and expert use the term "gender identity disorder", which was the term used by DSM-IV. In 2013, the American Psychiatric Association published DSM-V and replaced the "gender identity disorder" with "gender dysphoria" partly because, as explained by Dr. Kenneth Zucker, Chair of the DSM-5 Work Group on Sexual and Gender Identity Disorders, "some people didn't like the fact that the word 'disorder' was in the name of the diagnosis" and viewed it as "stigmatising." Kenneth J. Zucker & Robbie Duschinsky, *Dilemmas Encountered by the Sexual and Gender Identity Disorders Work Group for DSM-5: An Interview with Kenneth J. Zucker*, 7 PSYCH. & SEXUALITY 23 (2015). Dr. Zucker acknowledged the problem with including gender identity in the DSM at all—"a manual that ends with 'of mental disorders' "—and noted that the Work Group "debated the pros and cons of retention and deletion." *Id.* at 26. In the end, however, the "Work Group unanimously supported its retention in the DSM." *Id.* While members of the Work Group had different reasons for their decision, for at least one member, it was "primarily about access to care outweighing any other considerations." *Id*. Despite "mixed feelings" about continuing to include gender identity in the DSM, Dr. Zucker observed that:

> What you're really diagnosing is not gender identity per se but gender dysphoria, which is the disjunction between one's felt gender and somatic sex. And in that respect I like the term 'Gender Dysphoria' because it is capturing phenomenology. A patient comes to see you and they say they're in distress about a mismatch between their felt gender and their biological sex.

Id. The Work Group also considered using the term "Gender Incongruence" but received feedback "that it was too vague and it could potentially be misinterpreted." *Id*. What are the consequences of retaining gender identity in the DSM? Is the term "gender dysphoria" less stigmatizing than "gender identity disorder"? What do you make of the idea of retaining gender identity in the DSM as a means of accessing needed medical care?

3. Dr. Mark King, the expert who conducted the psychological evaluations in *Smith*, testified that the mother's decision to treat the child "as if he were a girl and as if he had GID was a mistake." He admitted, however, that "he could not give a diagnosis as to whether the boy suffered from GID", stating only (and not unproblematically) that "the child was a very feminized male" and that "this was the most difficult case he had ever dealt with." *Smith*, *supra*. Dr. King and the trial court considered only two options—the child was either a boy or a transgender girl. Is it possible that the child might identify as non-binary? Marie-Amélie George has noted that "when a child does not exhibit all of the gender stereotypes of their claimed identity, parents often argue that this establishes that the child is not transgender or gender expansive.*" Marie-Amélie George, *Exploring Identity*, 54 FAM. L.Q. 1, 12 (2021). In her view,

> [T]hese parents' arguments about their gender expansive children are problematic . . . because they fail to recognize that gender exists beyond male and female. Gender is a spectrum, with identities that may range between male and female. Individuals may also be nonbinary, agender, or have some other type of gender expansive identity.

Id. at 13.

4. For other decisions awarding custody to a parent who does not support the child's transgender identity, see *Paul E. v. Courtney F.*, 439 P.3d 1169 (Ariz. 2019); *Williams v. Frymire*, 377 S.W.3d 579 (Ky. Ct. App. 2012); *Schrader v. Spain*, No. 05–95–01649–CV, 1998 WL 40632, at *2 (Tex. App. Feb. 4, 1998). *But see Kristen L. v. Benjamin W.*, No. S–15302, 2014 WL 2716842, at *2 (Alaska June 11, 2014) (affirming trial court's modification of custody to the father in part because of the mother's "inability to deal with her child's transgender issue"); *In re Churchill/Belinski*, No. 337790, 2018 WL 1343986, at *3 (Mich. Ct. App. Mar. 15, 2018) (concluding that "forcing a child to act as a gender the child does not identify with—whatever gender

---

* Ed. Note: Professor George uses the term "gender expansive children" to "refer to transgender and nonbinary children, as well as children exploring nontraditional gender identities." Marie-Amélie George, *Exploring Identity*, 54 FAM. L.Q. 1, 1 (2021).

that is, and whatever gender the parent is attempting to coerce—is certainly the kind of mistreatment by a parent that could cause deep and lasting harm to a child"), *rev'd in part, appeal denied in part*, 919 N.W.2d 285 (Mich. 2018). *See also* George, *supra*, at 28 Table 1. For discussion of the challenges faced by mothers who affirm the child's gender identity over the objections of the child's father, see Katherine A, Kuvalanka et al., *An Exploratory Study of Custody Challenges Experienced by Affirming Mothers of Transgender and Gender-Nonconforming Children*, 57 FAM. CT. REV. 54 (2019).

5. Children may suffer emotional harm as a result of parental rejection of the child's sexual orientation or gender identity and expression. Some parents attempt to alter the child's sexual orientation or gender identity through counseling or other measures known as sexual orientation and gender identity conversion therapy. Several states and the District of Columbia have passed legislation prohibiting mental health professionals from engaging in efforts to change a child's sexual orientation and gender identity. *See, e.g.*, CAL. BUS. & PROF. CODE § 865.1 (West 2013); CONN. GEN. STAT. ANN. § 19a–907a (West 2017); D.C. CODE ANN. § 7–1231.14a (West 2019); 405 ILL. COMP. STAT. ANN. 48/20 (West 2016); NEV. REV. STAT. ANN. § 629.600 (West 2018); N.J. STAT. ANN. § 45:1–55 (West 2013); N.M. STAT. ANN. § 61–1–3.3 (West 2017); OR. REV. STAT. ANN. § 675.850 (West 2022); VT. STAT. ANN. tit. 18, § 8352 (West 2016). For cases rejecting constitutional challenges to statutes prohibiting conversion therapy on minors, see *Pickup v. Brown*, 740 F.3d 1208, 1236 (9th Cir. 2014) (concluding that parents do not have a fundamental right "to choose a specific type of provider for a specific medical or mental-health treatment that the state has reasonably deemed harmful"); *King v. Governor of the State of New Jersey*, 767 F.3d 216, 221 (3d Cir. 2014) (holding that licensed counselors lacked standing to assert that statute violated their minor clients' rights to free speech and free exercise of religion). Other states, however, have taken the position that providing a transgender minor with gender affirming treatment is child abuse. *See* Brad Brooks, *Texas Investigating Parents of Transgender Youth for Child Abuse*, REUTERS (Mar. 1, 2022), https://www.reuters.com/world/us/texas-investigating-parents-transgender-youth-child-abuse-2022-03-02/. *But see A Judge Blocks Texas from Investigating Families of Trans Youth*, ASSOCIATED PRESS (June 10, 2022), https://www.npr.org/2022/06/10/1104343876/judge-blocks-texas-investigating-families-trans-youth. Within days of the Supreme Court's decision in *Dobbs v. Jackson Women's Health, see* Chapter 3, *supra*, Alabama state officials argued that the decision supports its position that states can deny transgender minors access to gender affirming medical treatment. *See Alabama is Using the Case That Ended Roe to Argue it Can Ban Gender-Affirming Care*, ASSOCIATED PRESS (July 3, 2022), https://www.npr.org/2022/07/03/1109613520/alabama-abortion-rights-gender-affirming-care-law.

I. DE FACTO PARENTS

On page 1083 of the Unabridged 7th edition, and on page 739 of the Concise 7th edition, add the following note after note 4 and renumber note 5 to note 6:

5.   Michael Conover, the appellant in *Conover*, is a transgender man. He was in the process of gender transition at the time of the divorce. He was identified by his former name, "Michelle," at the hearing in the trial court, but by the time the case reached the Court of Appeals, he had changed his name to Michael. Although the *Conover* court acknowledged Michael's transition, it explained that it would continue to use female pronouns and Michael's former name to maintain consistency with the record as Michael had agreed to refer to himself by his former name and had stated in his brief that his gender identity was not relevant to the issues on appeal. Michael and his lawyer made this decision to avoid any risk that Michael's gender identity would obscure the legal issues in the case, which included both de facto parentage and another issue: whether the provision of Maryland's parentage statute establishing who is the "father" of a child should be given a gender-neutral interpretation, such that Michael would be legally presumed to be Jaxon's "father" under the statute (the court chose not to reach this issue in its decision, given its resolution of the appeal on the basis of de facto parentage). Michael and his lawyer feared that if the court focused on Michael's gender identity as male, it might misapprehend his claim for a gender-neutral interpretation of the parentage statute or might simply decline to consider the case at all. Telephone Interview with Jer Welter, counsel for Michael Conover (June 9, 2021). While this litigation strategy was successful, is there a dignitary cost to litigating under a "deadname" and incorrect gender identity? At the hearing, the parties introduced evidence that:

- Brittany took on the more "female" role in the relationship, while Michelle [now Michael] took on the more "masculine" role;

- Although Brittany later objected to the practice, Jaxon, at times, called Michelle [now Michael] "Dada" or "Daddy";

- Brittany sometimes referred to Michelle [now Michael] as Jaxon's father[.]

Conover, supra. In addition, at the hearing Michael argued that "although not a male, [he] has sufficiently satisfied three of the four criteria under" the parentage statute which, at the time, established that a person is a child's "father" if the person "(2) Has acknowledged himself, in writing, to be the father; (3) Has openly and notoriously recognized the child to be his child; or (4) Has subsequently married the mother and has acknowledged himself, orally or in writing, to be the father." *Id.* (citing MD. CODE, EST. & TRUSTS § 1–208(b)). (In 2019, after *Conover* was decided, the statute was amended to make it expressly gender-neutral.) Finally, Michael argued that "Brittany was estopped to deny that Michelle [now Michael] was the child's father." *Id.* Does this evidence challenge the assertion that Michael's gender identity was not relevant to this dispute?

On remand, the trial court found that Michael was Jaxon's legal father and was also a de facto parent. The court awarded the parties joint legal custody with primary physical custody to Brittany with visitation every other weekend to Michael. Official Partial Transcript of Proceedings at 13, *Eckel v. Conover*, No. 21–C–13–46273 (Cir. Ct. Wash. Cnty., Md. Feb. 16, 2017).

6.   Consider the requirements for establishing de facto parentage under the Uniform Parentage Act (UPA) excerpted below. What are the differences between the UPA's standard and the standard adopted by the Court of Appeals of Maryland in *Conover v. Conover*? Which standard would you prefer if you were representing the child who is the subject of the custody or visitation dispute? If you were representing the adoptive or biological parent? If you were representing the individual claiming to be a de facto parent?

CHAPTER 10

FAMILY LAW JURISDICTION, RECOGNITION, AND CHOICE OF LAW

D. CUSTODY JURISDICTION

2. INTERNATIONAL CUSTODY DISPUTES

On page 1314 of the Unabridged 7th edition, and on page 902 of the Concise 7th edition, after note 2, insert the following:

Monasky v. Taglieri

Supreme Court of the United States, 2020.
___ U.S. ___, 140 S.Ct. 719, 206 L.Ed.2d 9.

■ JUSTICE GINSBURG delivered the opinion of the Court.

Under the Hague Convention on the Civil Aspects of International Child Abduction (Hague Convention or Convention), Oct. 25, 1980, T. I. A. S. No. 11670, S. Treaty Doc. No. 99–11 (Treaty Doc.), a child wrongfully removed from her country of "habitual residence" ordinarily must be returned to that country. This case concerns the standard for determining a child's "habitual residence" and the standard for reviewing that determination on appeal. The petitioner, Michelle Monasky, is a U.S. citizen who brought her infant daughter, A.M.T., to the United States from Italy after her Italian husband, Domenico Taglieri, became abusive to Monasky. Taglieri successfully petitioned the District Court for A.M.T.'s return to Italy under the Convention, and the Court of Appeals affirmed the District Court's order.

Monasky assails the District Court's determination that Italy was A.M.T.'s habitual residence. First of the questions presented: Could Italy qualify as A.M.T.'s "habitual residence" in the absence of an actual agreement by her parents to raise her there? The second question: Should the Court of Appeals have reviewed the District Court's habitual-residence determination independently rather than deferentially? In accord with decisions of the courts of other countries party to the Convention, we hold that a child's habitual residence depends on the totality of the circumstances specific to the case. An actual agreement between the parents is not necessary to establish an infant's habitual residence. We further hold that a first-instance habitual-residence determination is subject to deferential appellate review for clear error.

I

A

The Hague Conference on Private International Law adopted the Hague Convention in 1980 "[t]o address the problem of international child abductions during domestic disputes." *Lozano v. Montoya Alvarez*, 572 U.S. 1, 4, 134 S.Ct. 1224, 188 L.Ed.2d 200 (2014). One hundred one countries, including the United States and Italy, are Convention signatories. . . . The International Child Abduction Remedies Act (ICARA), 102 Stat. 437, as amended, 22 U.S.C. § 9001 *et seq.*, implements our Nation's obligations under the Convention. It is the Convention's core premise that "the interests of children . . . in matters relating to their custody" are best served when custody decisions are made in the child's country of "habitual residence." Convention Preamble, Treaty Doc., at 7. . .

To that end, the Convention ordinarily requires the prompt return of a child wrongfully removed or retained away from the country in which she habitually resides. Art. 12, Treaty Doc., at 9 . . . The removal or retention is wrongful if done in violation of the custody laws of the child's habitual residence. Art. 3, *ibid.* The Convention recognizes certain exceptions to the return obligation. Prime among them, a child's return is not in order if the return would place her at a "grave risk" of harm or otherwise in "an intolerable situation." Art. 13(*b*), *id.*, at 10.

The Convention's return requirement is a "provisional" remedy that fixes the forum for custody proceedings. . . . Upon the child's return, the custody adjudication will proceed in that forum. To avoid delaying the custody proceeding, the Convention instructs contracting states to "use the most expeditious procedures available" to return the child to her habitual residence. Art. 2, Treaty Doc., at 7. See also Art. 11, *id.*, at 9 (prescribing six weeks as normal time for return-order decisions).

B

In 2011, Monasky and Taglieri were married in the United States. Two years later, they relocated to Italy, where they both found work. Neither then had definite plans to return to the United States. During their first year in Italy, Monasky and Taglieri lived together in Milan. But the marriage soon deteriorated. Taglieri became physically abusive, Monasky asserts, and "forced himself upon [her] multiple times." 907 F.3d 404, 406 (CA6 2018) (en banc).

About a year after their move to Italy, in May 2014, Monasky became pregnant. Taglieri thereafter took up new employment in the town of Lugo, while Monasky, who did not speak Italian, remained about three hours away in Milan. The long-distance separation and a difficult pregnancy further strained their marriage. Monasky looked into returning to the United States. She applied for jobs there, asked about U.S. divorce lawyers, and obtained cost information from moving companies. At the same time, though, she and Taglieri made preparations to care for their expected child in Italy. They inquired about childcare options there, made purchases needed for their baby to live in Italy, and found a larger apartment in a Milan suburb.

Their daughter, A.M.T., was born in February 2015. Shortly thereafter, Monasky told Taglieri that she wanted to divorce him, a matter they had previously broached, and that she anticipated returning to the United States. Later, however, she agreed to join Taglieri, together with A.M.T., in Lugo. The parties dispute whether they reconciled while together in that town.

On March 31, 2015, after yet another heated argument, Monasky fled with her daughter to the Italian police and sought shelter in a safe house. In a written statement to the police, Monasky alleged that Taglieri had abused her and that she feared for her life. Two weeks later, in April 2015, Monasky and two-month-old A.M.T. left Italy for Ohio, where they moved in with Monasky's parents.

Taglieri sought recourse in the courts. With Monasky absent from the proceedings, an Italian court granted Taglieri's request to terminate Monasky's parental rights, discrediting her statement to the Italian police. In the United States, on May 15, 2015, Taglieri petitioned the U.S. District Court for the Northern District of Ohio for the return of A.M.T. to Italy under the Hague Convention . . . on the ground that Italy was her habitual residence.

The District Court granted Taglieri's petition after a four-day bench trial. Sixth Circuit precedent at the time, the District Court observed, instructed courts that a child habitually resides where the child has become "acclimatiz[ed]" to her surroundings. . . . An infant, however, is "too young" to acclimate to her surroundings. The District Court therefore proceeded on the assumption that "the shared intent of the [parents] is relevant in determining the habitual residence of an infant," though "particular facts and circumstances . . . might necessitate the consideration [of] other factors." The shared intention of A.M.T.'s parents, the District Court found, was for their daughter to live in Italy, where the parents had established a marital home "with no definitive plan to return to the United States." Even if Monasky could change A.M.T.'s habitual residence unilaterally by making plans to raise A.M.T. away from Italy, the District Court added, the evidence on that score indicated that, until the day she fled her husband, Monasky had "no definitive plans" to raise A.M.T. in the United States. In line with its findings, the District Court ordered A.M.T.'s prompt return to Italy.

The Sixth Circuit and this Court denied Monasky's requests for a stay of the return order pending appeal. In December 2016, A.M.T., nearly two years old, was returned to Italy and placed in her father's care.[1]

_____

[1] Taglieri represents that "[a]n order issued by the Italian court in December 2018 awarded legal custody of A.M.T., on an interim basis, to the Lugo municipality . . . with

In the United States, Monasky's appeal of the District Court's return order proceeded. See *Chafin v. Chafin*, 568 U.S. 165, 180, 133 S.Ct. 1017, 185 L.Ed.2d 1 (2013) (the return of a child under the Hague Convention does not moot an appeal of the return order). A divided three-judge panel of the Sixth Circuit affirmed the District Court's order, and a divided en banc court adhered to that disposition.

. . .

We granted certiorari to clarify the standard for habitual residence, an important question of federal and international law, in view of differences in emphasis among the Courts of Appeals. . . . Certiorari was further warranted to resolve a division in Courts of Appeals over the appropriate standard of appellate review. . . .

II

The first question presented concerns the standard for habitual residence: Is an actual agreement between the parents on where to raise their child categorically necessary to establish an infant's habitual residence? We hold that the determination of habitual residence does not turn on the existence of an actual agreement.

A

. . . The Hague Convention does not define the term "habitual residence." A child "resides" where she lives. See Black's Law Dictionary 1176 (5th ed. 1979). Her residence in a particular country can be deemed "habitual," however, only when her residence there is more than transitory. "Habitual" implies "[c]ustomary, usual, of the nature of a habit." *Id.*, at 640. The Hague Convention's text alone does not definitively tell us what makes a child's residence sufficiently enduring to be deemed "habitual." It surely does not say that habitual residence depends on an actual agreement between a child's parents. But the term "habitual" does suggest a fact-sensitive inquiry, not a categorical one.

The Convention's explanatory report confirms what the Convention's text suggests. The report informs that habitual residence is a concept "well-established . . . in the Hague Conference." . . . The report refers to a child's habitual residence in fact-focused terms: "the family and social environment in which [the child's] life has developed." . . . What makes a child's residence "habitual" is therefore "some degree of integration by the child in a social and family environment." . . . The place where a child is at home, at the time of removal or retention, ranks as the child's habitual residence. . . .

Because locating a child's home is a fact-driven inquiry, courts must be "sensitive to the unique circumstances of the case and informed by common sense." [*Redmond v. Redmond*, 724 F.3d 729, 744 (7th Cir. 2013)]. For older children capable of acclimating to their surroundings,

---

placement at [Taglieri's] residence; and provided that mother-daughter visits would continue under the plan prescribed in a court order issued earlier in 2018." . . .

courts have long recognized, facts indicating acclimatization will be highly relevant.[3] Because children, especially those too young or otherwise unable to acclimate, depend on their parents as caregivers, the intentions and circumstances of caregiving parents are relevant considerations. No single fact, however, is dispositive across all cases. Common sense suggests that some cases will be straightforward: Where a child has lived in one place with her family indefinitely, that place is likely to be her habitual residence. But suppose, for instance, that an infant lived in a country only because a caregiving parent had been coerced into remaining there. Those circumstances should figure in the calculus. . . .

The treaty's "negotiation and drafting history" corroborates that a child's habitual residence depends on the specific circumstances of the particular case. . . . The Convention's explanatory report states that the Hague Conference regarded habitual residence as "a question of pure fact, differing in that respect from domicile.". . . The Conference deliberately chose "habitual residence" for its factual character, making it the foundation for the Convention's return remedy in lieu of formal legal concepts like domicile and nationality. . . . That choice is instructive. The signatory nations sought to afford courts charged with determining a child's habitual residence "maximum flexibility" to respond to the particular circumstances of each case. . . . The aim: to ensure that custody is adjudicated in what is presumptively the most appropriate forum—the country where the child is at home.

Our conclusion that a child's habitual residence depends on the particular circumstances of each case is bolstered by the views of our treaty partners. ICARA expressly recognizes "the need for uniform international interpretation of the Convention." 22 U.S.C. § 9001(b)(3)(B) . . . The understanding that the opinions of our sister signatories to a treaty are due "considerable weight," this Court has said, has "special force" in Hague Convention cases. . . . The "clear trend" among our treaty partners is to treat the determination of habitual residence as a fact-driven inquiry into the particular circumstances of the case. . . .

. . . Tellingly, Monasky has not identified a single treaty partner that has adopted her actual-agreement proposal. . . .

The bottom line: There are no categorical requirements for establishing a child's habitual residence—least of all an actual-agreement requirement for infants. Monasky's proposed actual-agreement requirement is not only unsupported by the Convention's text and inconsistent with the leeway and international harmony the

---

[3] Facts courts have considered include: "a change in geography combined with the passage of an appreciable period of time," "age of the child," "immigration status of child and parent," "academic activities," "social engagements," "participation in sports programs and excursions," "meaningful connections with the people and places in the child's new country," "language proficiency," and "location of personal belongings." Federal Judicial Center, J. Garbolino, The 1980 Hague Convention on the Civil Aspects of International Child Abduction: A Guide for Judges 67–68 (2d ed. 2015).

Convention demands; her proposal would thwart the Convention's "objects and purposes." . . . An actual-agreement requirement would enable a parent, by withholding agreement, unilaterally to block any finding of habitual residence for an infant. If adopted, the requirement would undermine the Convention's aim to stop unilateral decisions to remove children across international borders. Moreover, when parents' relations are acrimonious, as is often the case in controversies arising under the Convention, agreement can hardly be expected. In short, as the Court of Appeals observed below, "Monasky's approach would create a presumption of no habitual residence for infants, leaving the population most vulnerable to abduction the least protected." 907 F.3d at 410.

B

Monasky counters that an actual-agreement requirement is necessary to ensure "that an infant's mere physical presence in a country has a sufficiently settled quality to be deemed 'habitual.' " . . . An infant's "mere physical presence," we agree, is not a dispositive indicator of an infant's habitual residence. But a wide range of facts other than an actual agreement, including facts indicating that the parents have made their home in a particular place, can enable a trier to determine whether an infant's residence in that place has the quality of being "habitual."

Monasky also argues that a bright-line rule like her proposed actual-agreement requirement would promote prompt returns of abducted children and deter would-be abductors from "tak[ing] their chances" in the first place. . . . Adjudicating a winner-takes-all evidentiary dispute over whether an agreement existed, however, is scarcely more expeditious than providing courts with leeway to make "a quick impression gained on a panoramic view of the evidence." . . . When all the circumstances are in play, would-be abductors should find it more, not less, difficult to manipulate the reality on the ground, thus impeding them from forging "artificial jurisdictional links . . . with a view to obtaining custody of a child." . . . .

Finally, Monasky and *amici curiae* raise a troublesome matter: An actual-agreement requirement, they say, is necessary to protect children born into domestic violence. . . . Domestic violence poses an "intractable" problem in Hague Convention cases involving caregiving parents fleeing with their children from abuse. . . . We doubt, however, that imposing a categorical actual-agreement requirement is an appropriate solution, for it would leave many infants without a habitual residence, and therefore outside the Convention's domain. . . . Settling the forum for adjudication of a dispute over a child's custody, of course, does not dispose of the merits of the controversy over custody. Domestic violence should be an issue fully explored in the custody adjudication upon the child's return.

The Hague Convention, we add, has a mechanism for guarding children from the harms of domestic violence. . . . Article 13(b) allows a court to refrain from ordering a child's return to her habitual residence if "there is a grave risk that [the child's] return would expose the child to physical or psychological harm or otherwise place the child in an intolerable situation." . . . Monasky raised below an Article 13(b) defense to Taglieri's return petition. In response, the District Court credited Monasky's "deeply troubl[ing]" allegations of her exposure to Taglieri's physical abuse. . . . But the District Court found "no evidence" that Taglieri ever abused A.M.T. or otherwise disregarded her well-being. . . . That court also followed Circuit precedent disallowing consideration of psychological harm A.M.T. might experience due to separation from her mother. . . . Monasky does not challenge those dispositions in this Court.

III

Turning to the second question presented: What is the appropriate standard of appellate review of an initial adjudicator's habitual-residence determination? Neither the Convention nor ICARA prescribes modes of appellate review, other than the directive to act "expeditiously." . . .

. . .

A child's habitual residence presents what U.S. law types a "mixed question" of law and fact—albeit barely so. . . . The inquiry begins with a legal question: What is the appropriate standard for habitual residence? Once the trial court correctly identifies the governing totality-of-the-circumstances standard, however, what remains for the court to do in applying that standard . . . is to answer a factual question: Was the child at home in the particular country at issue? The habitual-residence determination thus presents a task for factfinding courts, not appellate courts, and should be judged on appeal by a clear-error review standard deferential to the factfinding court.

. . .

Clear-error review has a particular virtue in Hague Convention cases. As a deferential standard of review, clear-error review speeds up appeals and thus serves the Convention's premium on expedition. . . .

IV

Although agreeing with the manner in which the Court has resolved the two questions presented, the United States, as an *amicus curiae* supporting neither party, suggests remanding to the Court of Appeals rather than affirming that court's judgment. . . . Ordinarily, we might take that course, giving the lower courts an opportunity to apply the governing totality-of-the-circumstances standard in the first instance.

Under the circumstances of this case, however, we decline to disturb the judgment below. True, the lower courts viewed A.M.T.'s situation through the lens of her parents' shared intentions. But, after a four-day bench trial, the District Court had before it all the facts relevant to the dispute. . . .

Monasky does urge the Court to reverse if it rests A.M.T.'s habitual residence on all relevant circumstances. She points to her "absence of settled ties to Italy" and the "unsettled and unstable conditions in which

A.M.T. resided in Italy." . . . The District Court considered the competing facts bearing on those assertions, however, including the fraught circumstances in which the parties' marriage unraveled. That court nevertheless found that Monasky had sufficient ties to Italy such that "[a]rguably, [she] was a habitual resident of Italy." . . . And, despite the rocky state of the marriage, the District Court found beyond question that A.M.T. was born into "a marital home in Italy," one that her parents established "with no definitive plan to return to the United States." . . . Nothing in the record suggests that the District Court would appraise the facts differently on remand.

A remand would consume time when swift resolution is the Convention's objective. The instant return-order proceedings began a few months after A.M.T.'s birth. She is now five years old. The more than four-and-a-half-year duration of this litigation dwarfs the six-week target time for resolving a return-order petition. . . . Taglieri represents that custody of A.M.T. has so far been resolved only "on an interim basis," . . . and that custody proceedings, including the matter of Monasky's parental rights, remain pending in Italy. . . . Given the exhaustive record before the District Court, the absence of any reason to anticipate that the District Court's judgment would change on a remand that neither party seeks, and the protraction of proceedings thus far, final judgment on A.M.T.'s return is in order.

* * *

For the reasons stated, the judgment of the Court of Appeals for the Sixth Circuit is

Affirmed.

■ JUSTICE THOMAS, concurring in part and concurring in the judgment.

The Court correctly concludes that an actual agreement between parents is not necessary to establish the habitual residence of an infant who is too young to acclimatize. . . . I also agree with the Court's conclusion that the habitual-residence inquiry is intensely fact driven, requiring courts to take account of the unique circumstances of each case. I write separately, however, because I would decide this case principally on the plain meaning of the treaty's text.

I

. . . .

" 'The interpretation of a treaty, like the interpretation of a statute, begins with its text.' " *Abbott v. Abbott*, 560 U.S. 1, 10, 130 S.Ct. 1983, 176 L.Ed.2d 789 (2010) . . . . The Court recognizes this fact, but it concludes that the text only "suggests" that habitual residence is a fact-driven inquiry, and ultimately relies on atextual sources to "confir[m] what the Convention's text suggests." . . . In my view, the ordinary meaning of the relevant language at the time of the treaty's enactment provides strong evidence that the habitual-residence inquiry is inherently fact driven. . . .

In 1980, as today, "habitual" referred to something that was "[c]ustomary" or "usual." Black's Law Dictionary 640 (5th ed. 1979); see also 6 Oxford English Dictionary 996 (2d ed. 1989) ("existing as a settled practice or condition; constantly repeated or continued; customary"); Webster's Third New International Dictionary 1017 (1976) (similar). And "residence" referred to a "[p]ersonal presence at some place of abode," Black's Law Dictionary, at 1176, "one's usual dwelling-place," 13 Oxford English Dictionary, at 707, or "the act or fact of abiding or dwelling in a place for some time," Webster's Third New International Dictionary, at 1931; see also ibid. ("a temporary or permanent dwelling place, abode, or habitation").

These definitions demonstrate that the concept of habitual residence for a child too young to acclimatize cannot be reduced to a neat set of necessary and sufficient conditions. Answering the question of what is customary or usual, for instance, requires judges to consider a host of facts, such as the presence or absence of bank accounts and driver's licenses, the length and type of employment, and the strength and duration of other community ties. Determining whether there is a residence involves the consideration of factors such as the presence or absence of a permanent home, the duration in the country at issue, and, in some cases, an actual agreement between the parents to reside in a particular place. Accordingly, the ordinary meaning of the phrase "habitual residence" provides strong support for the conclusion that an objective agreement between the child's parents is not required. This plain meaning should serve as the primary guide for our interpretation. . . .

II

This case exemplifies the wisdom of firmly anchoring our discussion in the text before turning to the decisions of sister signatories—especially when those decisions are not contemporaneous with the treaty's passage. . . .

. . .

. . . I would rely on the plain meaning of "habitual residence" to conclude that an actual agreement is not necessary. . . . Because the Court places insufficient weight on the treaty's text, I cannot join Part II of its opinion.

■ JUSTICE ALITO, concurring in part and concurring in the judgment.

I agree with the Court on almost all the issues in this case. . . . I also agree with Justice THOMAS that we must independently interpret the meaning of "habitual residence."

So what does it mean? The term "habitual" is used to refer to a cluster of related concepts. It can be used to refer to things done by habit, as well as things that are "constantly repeated or continued," "usual," or "accustomed." 6 Oxford English Dictionary 996 (2d ed. 1989) . . . . If taken in isolation, each of these understandings might lead to a different analysis in applying the concept of "habitual residence" under the Convention. . . . But I think the Court accurately captures what the term means under the Convention when it says that a child's habitual residence is the child's "home.". . .

Of course the concept of "home" is also multifaceted. It can be used to signify the place where a person generally sleeps, eats, works, and engages in social and recreational activities, but it can also mean the place where a person feels most comfortable and the place to which the person has the strongest emotional ties. . . . As best I can determine, the concept of "habitual residence" under the Convention embraces all of these meanings to some degree. If forced to try to synthesize them, I would say it means the place where the child in fact has been living for an extended period—unless that place was never regarded as more than temporary or there is another place to which the child has a strong attachment. I think this is the core of what courts have made of the concept of "habitual residence," and it appears to represent the best distillation of the various shades of meaning of the term taken in context.

So interpreted, "habitual residence" is not a pure question of fact, at least as we understand that concept in our legal system. But it does involve a heavily factual inquiry. For these reasons, I would say that the standard of review on appeal is abuse of discretion, not clear error. As a practical matter, the difference may be no more than minimal. The important point is that great deference should be afforded to the District Court's determination.

NOTES

1. Review the UCCJEA, *supra*. What are the similarities and differences between a child's "home state" under the UCCJEA and a child's "habitual residence" under the Hague Convention?

2. For discussion of the potential effects of *Monasky*, see Ann Laquer Estin, *Where Is the Child at Home? Determining Habitual Residence After Monasky*, 54 FAM. L.Q. 127 (2020).

3. The Court in *Monasky* concedes that "[d]omestic violence poses an 'intractable' problem in Hague Convention cases" but suggests that it should either be addressed by the country of the child's habitual residence once the child is returned or that the Convention's grave risk of harm exception is an adequate mechanism for protecting children from the harms of domestic violence. Consider the Court's decision in *Golan v. Saada*, below. Do you think that the grave risk of harm exception adequately protects children from the harms of domestic violence? What might *Abbott, supra, Charalambous, supra, Monasky, supra,* and *Golan, infra* teach us about courts' treatment of domestic violence against a parent in Hague Convention abduction cases?

Golan v. Saada

Supreme Court of the United States, 2022.
___ U.S. ___, 142 S.Ct. 1880, ___ L.Ed. ___.

■ JUSTICE SOTOMAYOR delivered the opinion of the Court.

Under the Hague Convention on the Civil Aspects of International Child Abduction, Mar. 26, 1986, T.I.A.S. No. 11670, S. Treaty Doc. No. 99–11 (Treaty Doc.), if a court finds that a child was wrongfully removed from the child's country of habitual residence, the court ordinarily must order the child's return. There are, however, exceptions to that rule. As relevant here, a court is not bound to order a child's return if it finds that return would put the child at a grave risk of physical or psychological harm. In such a circumstance, a court has discretion to determine whether to deny return.

In exercising this discretion, courts often consider whether any "ameliorative measures," undertaken either "by the parents" or "by the authorities of the state having jurisdiction over the question of custody," could "reduce whatever risk might otherwise be associated with a child's repatriation." *Blondin v. Dubois*, 189 F.3d 240, 248 (C.A.2 1999) (*Blondin I*). The Second Circuit has made such consideration a requirement, mandating that district courts independently "examine the full range of options that might make possible the safe return of a child" before denying return due to grave risk, even if the party petitioning for the child's return has not identified or argued for imposition of ameliorative measures. *Blondin v. Dubois*, 238 F.3d 153, 163, n. 11 (C.A.2 2001) (*Blondin II*).

The Second Circuit's categorical requirement to consider all ameliorative measures is inconsistent with the text and other express requirements of the Hague Convention.

I

A

The Hague Convention "was adopted in 1980 in response to the problem of international child abductions during domestic disputes." *Abbott v. Abbott*, 560 U.S. 1, 8 (2010). One hundred and one countries, including the United States and Italy, are signatories. . . .

The Convention's "core premise" is that " 'the interests of children . . . in matters relating to their custody' are best served when custody decisions are made in the child's country of 'habitual residence.' " *Monasky v. Taglieri*, 589 U.S. ___, ___, 140 S.Ct. 719, 723 (2020) (quoting Convention Preamble, Treaty Doc., at 7). Accordingly, the Convention generally requires the "prompt return" of a child to the child's country of habitual residence when the child has been wrongfully removed to or retained in another country. Art. 1(a), Treaty Doc., at 7; see also Art. 12, *id.,* at 9.[1] This requirement "ensure[s] that rights of custody and of access under the law of one Contracting State are effectively respected in the other Contracting States." Art. 1(b), *id.,* at 7. Return of the child is, however, a general rule, and there are exceptions. As relevant here, the Convention provides that return is not required if "[t]here is a grave risk that . . . return would expose the child to physical or psychological harm or otherwise place the child in an intolerable situation." Art. 13(b), *id.,* at 10.[2] Because return is merely "a 'provisional' remedy that fixes the forum for custody proceedings," *Monasky,* 589 U.S., at ___, 140 S.Ct., at 723, the Convention requires that the determination as to whether to order return should be made "us[ing] the most expeditious procedures available," Art. 2, Treaty Doc., at 7; see also Art. 11, *id.,* at 9 (providing that the party petitioning for return has "the right to request a statement of the reasons for the delay" if the court "has not reached a decision within six weeks from the date of commencement of the proceedings"). Congress implemented the Convention in the International Child Abduction Remedies Act (ICARA), 102 Stat. 437, as amended, 22 U.S.C. § 9001 *et seq.* ICARA permits a parent (or other individual or institution) seeking relief under the Convention to file a petition for return of a child in state or federal court, §§ 9003(a)–(b), and directs courts to "decide the[se] case[s] in accordance with the Convention," § 9003(d). Consistent with the Convention, ICARA "empower[s] courts in the United States to determine only rights under the Convention and not the merits of any underlying child custody claims." § 9001(b)(4) . . . .

Under ICARA, the party petitioning for the child's return bears the burden of establishing by a preponderance of the evidence that the child was wrongfully removed or retained. § 9003(e)(1). If the court finds the child was wrongfully removed or retained, the respondent opposing return of the child has the burden of establishing that an exception to the return requirement applies. § 9003(e)(2). A respondent arguing that return would expose the child to a grave risk of harm must establish that this exception applies by "clear and convincing evidence." § 9003(e)(2)(A). Absent a finding that an exception applies, a child determined to be wrongfully removed or retained must be "promptly returned" to the child's country of habitual residence. § 9001(a)(4).

---

[1]   The Convention defines a "wrongful" removal or retention as one that breaches existing custody rights "under the law of the State in which the child was habitually resident immediately before the removal or retention" if those rights "were actually exercised" or "would have been so exercised but for the removal or retention." Art. 3, Treaty Doc., at 7.

[2]   The Convention also enumerates several other exceptions to the return requirement. Return is not required if the parent, institution, or body having care of the child seeking return was not exercising custody rights at the time of removal or had consented to removal, if the child objects to return and "has attained an age and degree of maturity at which it is appropriate to take account of its views," or if return would conflict with fundamental principles of freedom and human rights in the country from which return is requested. Arts. 13, 20, Treaty Doc., at 10, 11.

B

Petitioner Narkis Golan is a citizen of the United States. She met respondent Isacco Saada, an Italian citizen, while attending a wedding in Milan, Italy, in 2014. Golan soon moved to Milan, and the two wed in August 2015. Their son, B. A. S., was born the next summer in Milan, where the family lived for the first two years of B. A. S.' life.

The following facts, as found by the District Court, are not in dispute. Saada and Golan's relationship was characterized by violence from the beginning. The two fought on an almost daily basis and, during their arguments, Saada would sometimes push, slap, and grab Golan and pull her hair. Saada also yelled and swore at Golan and frequently insulted her and called her names, often in front of other people. Saada once told Golan's family that he would kill her. Much of Saada's abuse of Golan occurred in front of his son.

In July 2018, Golan flew with B. A. S. to the United States to attend her brother's wedding. Rather than return as scheduled in August, however, Golan moved into a domestic violence shelter with B. A. S. In September, Saada filed in Italy a criminal complaint for kidnapping and initiated a civil proceeding seeking sole custody of B. A. S.

Saada also filed a petition under the Convention and ICARA in the U.S. District Court for the Eastern District of New York, seeking an order for B. A. S.' return to Italy. The District Court granted Saada's petition after a 9-day bench trial. As a threshold matter, the court determined that Italy was B. A. S.' habitual residence and that Golan had wrongfully retained B. A. S. in the United States in violation of Saada's rights of custody. The court concluded, however, that returning B. A. S. to Italy would expose him to a grave risk of harm. The court observed that there was "no dispute" that Saada was "violent—physically, psychologically, emotionally, and verbally—to" Golan and that "B. A. S. was present for much of it." App. to Pet. for Cert. 79a. The court described some of the incidents B. A. S. had witnessed as "chilling." *Ibid.* While B. A. S. was not "the target of violence," undisputed expert testimony established that "domestic violence disrupts a child's cognitive and social-emotional development, and affects the structure and organization of the child's brain." *Id.*, at 79a–80a, and n. 37.[3] Records indicated that Italian social services, who had been involved with the couple while they lived in Italy, had also concluded that " 'the family situation entails a developmental danger' for B. A. S." *Id.*, at 80a. The court found that Saada had demonstrated no "capacity to change his behavior," explaining that Saada "minimized or tried to excuse his violent conduct" during his testimony and that Saada's "own expert said . . . that [Saada] could not control his anger or take responsibility for his behavior." *Ibid.*

---

    [3]   The court noted that "[t]here were isolated incidents of possible abuse" of B. A. S. based on Golan's testimony that Saada had inadvertently hit and pushed B. A. S. while targeting her and Golan's brother's testimony that Saada had spanked B. A. S. aggressively, accusations that Saada disputed. . . .

The court nonetheless ordered B. A. S.' return to Italy based on Second Circuit precedent obligating it to " 'examine the full range of options that might make possible the safe return of a child to the home country' " before it could " 'deny repatriation on the ground that a grave risk of harm exists.' " *Id.*, at 81a . . . . The Second Circuit based this rule on its view that the Convention requires return "if at all possible." *Blondin I*, 189 F.3d at 248. To comply with these precedents, the District Court had required the parties to propose " 'ameliorative measures' " that could enable B. A. S.' safe return. . . . Saada had proposed that he would provide Golan with $30,000 for expenses pending a decision in Italian courts as to financial support, stay away from Golan until the custody dispute was resolved, pursue dismissal of the criminal charges he had filed against Golan, begin cognitive behavioral therapy, and waive any right to legal fees or expenses under the Convention. The court concluded that these measures, combined with the fact that Saada and Golan would be living separately, would "reduce the occasions for violence," thereby ameliorating the grave risk to B. A. S. sufficiently to require his return. *Id.*, at 81a–82a.

On Golan's appeal of this return order, the Second Circuit vacated the order, finding the District Court's measures insufficient to mitigate the risk of harm to B. A. S. Emphasizing that the District Court's factual findings provided "ample reason to doubt that Mr. Saada will comply with these conditions," the Second Circuit concluded that "the District Court erred in granting the petition subject to (largely) unenforceable undertakings" without "sufficient guarantees of performance." 930 F.3d 533, 540, 542–543 (2019). Because the record did "not support the conclusion that there exist *no* protective measures sufficient to ameliorate the grave risk of harm B. A. S. faces if repatriated," the court remanded for the District Court to "consider whether there exist alternative ameliorative measures that are either enforceable by the District Court or supported by other sufficient guarantees of performance." *Id.,* at 543 (emphasis added).

To comply with the Second Circuit's directive, over the course of nine months, the District Court conducted "an extensive examination of the measures available to ensure B. A. S.'s safe return to Italy." App. to Pet. for Cert. 12a. The District Court directed the parties to appear for status conferences and to submit status reports and supplemental briefs, and the court corresponded with the U.S. Department of State and the Italian Ministry of Justice. At the court's instruction, the parties petitioned the Italian courts for a protective order, and the Italian court overseeing the underlying custody dispute issued a protective order barring Saada from approaching Golan for one year. In addition, the Italian court ordered that an Italian social services agency oversee Saada's parenting classes and therapy and that visits between Saada and B. A. S. be supervised. . . . The District Court concluded that these measures were sufficient to ameliorate the harm to B. A. S. and again granted Saada's petition for B. A. S.' return. It rejected Golan's argument that Saada could not be trusted to comply with a court order, expressing confidence in the Italian courts' abilities to enforce the protective order. The District Court additionally ordered Saada to pay Golan $150,000 to facilitate B. A. S.' return to Italy and to cover Golan's and B. A. S.' living costs while they resettled. The Second Circuit affirmed, concluding that the District Court did not clearly err in determining that Saada likely would comply with the Italian protective order, given his compliance with other court orders and the threat of enforcement by Italian authorities of its order. . . .

This Court granted certiorari to decide whether the Second Circuit properly required the District Court, after making a grave-risk finding, to examine a full range of possible ameliorative measures before reaching a decision as to whether to deny return, and to resolve a division in the lower courts regarding whether ameliorative measures must be considered after a grave-risk finding. . . .

II

A

. . . As described above, when "a child has been wrongfully removed or retained" from his country of habitual residence, Article 12 of the Hague Convention generally requires the deciding authority (here, a district court) to "order the return of the child." Treaty Doc., at 9. Under Article 13(b) of the Convention, however, a court "is not bound to order the return of the child" if the court finds that the party opposing return has established that return would expose the child to a "grave risk" of physical or psychological harm. . . . By providing that a court "is not bound" to order return upon making a grave-risk finding, Article 13(b) lifts the Convention's return requirement, leaving a court with the discretion to grant or deny return.

Nothing in the Convention's text either forbids or requires consideration of ameliorative measures in exercising this discretion. The Convention itself nowhere mentions ameliorative measures. Nor does ICARA, which, as relevant, instructs courts to "decide the case in accordance with the Convention" and accordingly leaves undisturbed the discretion recognized in the Convention. 22 U.S.C. § 9003(d). The longstanding interpretation of the Department of State offers further support for the view that the Convention vests a court with discretion to determine whether to order return if an exception to the return mandate applies. . . .

Unable to point to any explicit textual mandate that courts consider ameliorative measures, Saada's primary argument is that this requirement is implicit in the Convention's command that the court make a determination as to whether a grave risk of harm exists. Essentially, Saada argues that determining whether a grave risk of harm exists necessarily requires considering whether any ameliorative measures are available.

The question whether there is a grave risk, however, is separate from the question whether there are ameliorative measures that could mitigate that risk. That said, the question whether ameliorative measures would be appropriate or effective will often overlap considerably with the inquiry into whether a grave risk exists. . . . In many instances, a court may find it appropriate to consider both questions at once. For example, a finding of grave risk as to a part of a country where an epidemic rages may naturally lead a court simultaneously to consider whether return to another part of the country is feasible. The fact that a court may consider ameliorative measures concurrent with the grave-risk determination, however, does not mean that the Convention imposes a categorical requirement on a court to consider any or all ameliorative measures before denying return once it finds that a grave risk exists. . . . Under the Convention and ICARA, district courts' discretion to determine whether to return a child where doing so would pose a grave risk to the child includes the discretion whether to consider ameliorative measures that could ensure the child's safe return. The Second Circuit's rule, "in practice, rewrite[s] the treaty," *Lozano v. Montoya Alvarez*, 572 U.S. 1, 17, 134 S.Ct. 1224, 188 L.Ed.2d 200 (2014), by imposing an atextual, categorical requirement that courts consider all possible ameliorative measures in exercising this discretion, regardless of whether such consideration is consistent with the Convention's objectives (and, seemingly, regardless of whether the parties offered them for the court's consideration in the first place). . . .

B

While consideration of ameliorative measures is within a district court's discretion, "[d]iscretion is not whim." *Martin v. Franklin Capital Corp.*, 546 U.S. 132, 139 (2005). A "motion to a court's discretion is a motion, not to its inclination, but to its judgment; and its judgment is to be guided by sound legal principles." *Ibid.* (internal quotation marks and alteration omitted). As a threshold matter, a district court exercising its discretion is still responsible for addressing and responding to nonfrivolous arguments timely raised by the parties before it. While a district court has no obligation under the Convention to consider ameliorative measures that have not been raised by the parties, it ordinarily should address ameliorative measures raised by the parties or obviously suggested by the circumstances of the case, such as in the example of the localized epidemic. . . .

In addition, the court's consideration of ameliorative measures must be guided by the legal principles and other requirements set forth in the Convention and ICARA. The Second Circuit's rule, by instructing district courts to order return "if at all possible," improperly elevated return above the Convention's other objectives. . . . The Convention does not pursue return exclusively or at all costs. Rather, the Convention "is designed to protect the interests of children and their parents," *Lozano*, 572 U.S. at 19 (ALITO, J., concurring), and children's interests may point against return in some circumstances. Courts must remain conscious of this purpose, as well as the Convention's other objectives and requirements, which constrain courts' discretion to consider ameliorative measures in at least three ways.

First, any consideration of ameliorative measures must prioritize the child's physical and psychological safety. The Convention explicitly recognizes that the child's interest in avoiding physical or psychological harm, in addition to other interests, "may overcome the return remedy." *Id.*, at 16 (majority opinion) (cataloging interests). . . . A court may therefore decline to consider imposing ameliorative measures where it is clear that they would not work because the risk is so grave. Sexual abuse of a child is one example of an intolerable situation . . . . Other physical or psychological abuse, serious neglect, and domestic violence in the home may also constitute an obvious grave risk to the child's safety that could not readily be ameliorated. A court may also decline to consider imposing ameliorative measures where it reasonably expects that they will not be followed. . . .

Second, consideration of ameliorative measures should abide by the Convention's requirement that courts addressing return petitions do not usurp the role of the court that will adjudicate the underlying custody dispute. The Convention and ICARA prohibit courts from resolving any underlying custody dispute in adjudicating a return petition. . . . Accordingly, a court ordering ameliorative measures in making a return determination should limit those measures in time and scope to conditions that would permit safe return, without purporting to decide subsequent custody matters or weighing in on permanent arrangements. . . .

Third, any consideration of ameliorative measures must accord with the Convention's requirement that courts "act expeditiously in proceedings for the return of children." Art. 11, Treaty Doc., at 9. . . . Timely resolution of return petitions is important in part because return is a "provisional" remedy to enable final custody determinations to proceed. *Monasky*, 589 U.S., at ___, 140 S.Ct., at 723 . . . . The Convention also prioritizes expeditious determinations as being in the best interests of the child because "[e]xpedition will help minimize the extent to which uncertainty adds to the challenges confronting both parents and child." *Chafin v. Chafin*, 568 U.S. 165, 180 (2013). A requirement to "examine the full range of options that might make possible the safe return of a child," *Blondin II*, 238 F.3d at 163, n. 11, is in tension with this focus on expeditious resolution. In this case, for example, it took the District Court nine months to comply with the Second Circuit's directive on remand. Remember, the Convention requires courts to resolve return petitions "us[ing] the most expeditious procedures available," Art. 2, Treaty Doc., at 7, and to provide parties that request it with an explanation if proceedings extend longer than six weeks, Art. 11, *id.*, at 9. Courts should structure return proceedings with these instructions in mind. Consideration of ameliorative measures should not cause undue delay in resolution of return petitions. To summarize, although nothing in the Convention prohibits a district court from considering ameliorative measures, and such consideration often may be appropriate, a district court reasonably may decline to consider ameliorative measures that have not been raised by the parties, are unworkable, draw the court into determinations properly resolved in custodial proceedings, or risk overly prolonging return proceedings. The court may also find the grave risk so unequivocal, or the potential harm so severe, that ameliorative measures would be inappropriate. Ultimately, a district court must exercise its discretion to consider ameliorative measures in a manner consistent with its general obligation to address the parties' substantive arguments and its specific obligations under the Convention. A district court's compliance with these requirements is subject to review under an ordinary abuse-of-discretion standard.

III

The question now becomes how to resolve the instant case. . . .

Under the circumstances of this case, this Court concludes that remand is appropriate. The Convention requires courts to make a discretionary determination as to whether to order return after making a finding of grave risk. The District Court made a finding of grave risk, but never had the opportunity to engage in the discretionary inquiry as to whether to order or deny return under the correct legal standard. This Court cannot know whether the District Court would have exercised its discretion to order B. A. S.' return absent the Second Circuit's rule, which improperly weighted the scales in favor of return. Accordingly, it is appropriate to follow the ordinary course and allow the District Court to apply the proper legal standard in the first instance. . . .

. . .

The judgment of the United States Court of Appeals for the Second Circuit is vacated, and the case is remanded for further proceedings consistent with this opinion.

It is so ordered.

NOTES

1.   A study of Hague Convention child abduction federal appellate cases from July 2000 through January 2001 and July 2017 through January 2018 found that during both time periods, 78 percent of cases involved allegations of domestic violence. See Merle H. Weiner, *You Can and You Should: How Judges Can Apply the Hague Abduction Convention to Protect Victims of Domestic Violence*, 28 UCLA WOMEN's L.J. 223, 226 (2021). Abductors who allege they were victims of domestic violence face significant obstacles when defending against the alleged abuser's petition for the child's return to the

country of habitual residence, "including trial judges' misunderstandings about domestic violence, doubts about survivors' credibility, and unwarranted faith in protective measures." *Id.* at 228. How should the law address these obstacles?

2. *Golan* is the U.S. Supreme Court's fifth decision on the Hague Convention on the Civil Aspects of International Child Abduction. See *Monasky v. Taglieri, supra*; *Abbott v. Abbott, supra*; *Chafin v. Chafin*, 568 U.S. 165 (2013); *Lozano v. Montoya Alvarez*, 572 U.S. 1 (2014).